What People Are Saying About

ReFashion Workshop

ReFashion Workshop is an important book for our time as we look at what we might wear in a post-petroleum future.
Carroll Dunham, *National Geographic*

ReFashion Workshop is an incredible resource for anyone looking to shift their ways and make a positive impact on the environment through their fashion choices. The 23 practices outlined in the book are powerful guides that are both accessible and effective.
Sienna Martz, PETA

Beautiful message. Beautiful dresses. And *sustainable*? It's about time!
Barry Simon, United Nations Association, Southern California, USA

We rarely think about the impacts of the clothing we wear, and yet, the clothing industry is one of the most wasteful and chemically intensive industries we support in our daily lives. This book is a practical guide to help us change our "outfit" on life.
Ryland Engelhart, Kiss the Ground

ReFashion Workshop is a much-needed practical guidebook that empowers fashion lovers to make informed decisions and embrace a sustainable lifestyle. Courtney's passion and experience in eco fashion shines, and I think the practices in

this book will help elevate your quality of life while protecting the planet.

Adrian Grenier, actor and activist

In *ReFashion Workshop*, Courtney not only shows us she designs what she preaches; she makes it a meaningful way of life — and gives us an inspiring framework to practice slow fashion on our terms.

Part self-meditation, part all-in-one guide, *ReFashion Workshop* unpacks the issues in fashion without overwhelming, leaving you with the energy needed for real transformation.

Kasi Martin, freelance journalist & wardrobe stylist, *Peahen Studio*

ReFashion Workshop

The Planet-Healing Mindset

ReFashion Workshop

The Planet-Healing Mindset

Courtney Barriger

CHANGEMAKERS
BOOKS

London, UK
Washington, DC, USA

CollectiveInk

First published by Changemakers Books, 2025
Changemakers Books is an imprint of Collective Ink Ltd.,
Unit 11, Shepperton House, 89 Shepperton Road, London, N1 3DF
office@collectiveinkbooks.com
www.collectiveinkbooks.com
www.changemakers-books.com

For distributor details and how to order please visit the 'Ordering' section on our website.

Text copyright: Courtney Barriger 2023

ISBN: 978 1 80341 422 5
978 1 80341 423 2 (ebook)
Library of Congress Control Number: 2023948039

A CIP catalogue record for this book is available from the British Library.

Cover artwork by Courtney Barriger
Design: Lapiz Digital Services

UK: Printed and bound by CPI Group (UK) Ltd, Croydon, CR0 4YY
Printed in North America by CPI GPS partners

We operate a distinctive and ethical publishing philosophy in all areas of our business, from our global network of authors to production and worldwide distribution.

Contents

Previous Books

NightBook Short Story Anthology
B005WQM9II

Sleepwalk to the Face
B00CM2RZYI

I dedicate this book to you, reader. All across the globe, in every culture and every country, we are opening our eyes to the power of our personal impact. Whenever I meet like-minded souls I am filled with joy, because in this endeavor to remake our world it can feel overwhelming. The sheer size of the 'powers that be' can make you feel small and insignificant. Just the fact that you have chosen this book means we are taking back our power collectively. You are the hope for a better future, and I hope that this book empowers you to take on this challenge and realize just how important your thoughts and actions are to the whole. Thank you for your bravery. If you let it, this journey will change your life.

Foreword

Having a practical guidebook to inform and help those who love clothing make more aware decisions is something that is needed. The fashion industry undeniably impacts our planet in a negative way. Toxically made products, materials that don't biodegrade, things that generally are bad for the environment are also detrimental to your own health and your own quality of life. For me it's about increasing your awareness and your appreciation for the things that improve your quality of life.

I've seen Courtney at work in the eco fashion movement for years, and I know she has found the thing that inspires her to create and to elevate life around her. Find the things that inspire you and the products that are going to enrich your health and well-being. *ReFashion Workshop* is a great tool to start. From here, find your own way towards a sustainable lifestyle you love.

Adrian Grenier, actor and activist

Preface

What is *ReFashion Workshop*?

An aspirational title — but what does it mean exactly? ReFashion Workshop is a deep inquiry and rapid mindfulness integration of sustainable practices aimed at your wardrobe that I've developed over my years working as a designer in the fashion industry and in my personal pursuit of holistic wellness. It's a process I've used to get astounding results in building the link between the clothes you buy and their effect on the planet, its people, and yourself.

"ReFashioning" is a term I teach that dissolves negative purchasing habits. By being honest and transparent about what we buy and why, we can shift into a planet-healing mindset using tried-and-true happiness hacks.

And to be sure, you will be confronted. In an effort to make it clear that the need for change is dire, I have gathered testimony from scientists, activists, anthropologists, and even a few actors.

- You will read interviews that address everything from climate change, toxicity, fair wages, to where your thrown-away clothes really go.
- You will take surveys to determine your personal carbon footprint, your level of happiness, and more.
- You will join an online community to share your journey and have accountability.
- You will come to understand what drives your fashion habits, learn to ReFashion them, and become a steward of the Earth.

Nature is our most sacred place, and it is in trouble because humans have taken everything too far. We are all to blame for the downward turn of our planet's ecosystems. In the early days of my environmental inquiry, I exclusively blamed corporations for the detriment they cause the planet, but I did nothing to change my own buying habits.

For 15 years I worked as a model in the fashion industry, inadvertently helping fast-fashion brands make it in America. I was knee deep in cheap, fast-fashion freebies I had been given as a model for commercial brands in Los Angeles. And I found myself stuck in harmful patterns that didn't honor my highest value for the planet I love. So deeply ingrained were these patterns that for a long time I wasn't even aware of them. They affected my spending habits, my relationships with my family, my relationship with my beloved, and even the way that I was showing up in my presence or lack of presence in the world around me and my community. I was acting out of a strong desire to just fit in, to look the part of a fashionista with something new to wear out every day. But all of that changed when I had the opportunity to create my own fashion label, and started asking myself: "How can I do this better?"

I had to learn to ReFashion myself. In this book, I am sharing the practices in motion in my own life. I have experienced profound changes in how I embrace the fullness of myself — knowing myself more deeply, without judgment, than I ever have before, releasing my need to please others, and finding the ability to love other people and the planet with more integrity. And yes, all of this was connected to my lack of mindfulness in how I wanted to appear in the world, namely in how I used clothing to hide myself.

In the time since I ReFashioned my life I launched my sustainable and award-winning clothing line Holding Court Inc., which has been featured in *Vanity Fair* and *GQ*. I've had the honor of debuting my first sustainable label at the United Nations Fashion Fights Poverty Gala at the French Embassy in Washington, DC. I've been named "The Future of Fashion" as a designer. And my focus has shifted to sharing how I learned to ReFashion my toxic relationship with fashion, in order to help those who are curious shift their lifestyles to be more sustainable.

I find as I write this book on sustainability and mindfulness, I am reminded how much ReFashioning really is a practice. You don't one day have it totally figured out. Just as I am being gentle on myself, approaching ReFashioning daily as something imperfect, so should you as you open your heart and open your mind to discover how your actions have contributed to a decline in the global ecosystem and how a lack of mindfulness can keep you trapped in patterns that hold you back from experiencing the fullness of love and life.

So I invite you to soak up all the rich life-journeys that are recounted in the interviews in this book. These beautiful souls have each dedicated themselves to bettering the world, and I want to acknowledge their contribution and send a strong "thank you" their way. And I hope that you can commit to each practice within the book with personal accountability, curiosity, and a sense of excitement at who you will be on the other end of it.

These practices and interviews have changed my life, and I hope that they will have a positive impact on yours as well, so that you can discover your highest respect for nature by improving your relationship with what you wear — one mindful practice at a time.

— *Courtney Barriger*

1

Anthropocene

Enter the "Age of Man."

> *Anthropocene — from anthropo, for 'man,' and cene, for 'new' — because humankind has caused mass extinctions of plant and animal species, polluted the oceans and altered the atmosphere, among other lasting impacts.*
>
> — Smithsonian Mag

Have you ever said yes to something that could easily have been a no, only for it to change the course of your entire life?

I sat uncomfortably on a cold plastic chair in a drab casting office in Hollywood, California, with 40 other deadpan women, listening to an intriguing — yet messy — pitch for a reality TV show that focused on choosing America's next "It Girl." "This is your chance to become a star," the producer intoned excitedly, playing a slide show that featured Sandra Bullock from *Miss Congeniality*, "and all you have to do is be the entrepreneur you already are."

The premise was some sort of combination of *Project Runway* meets *America's Next Top Model* meets, I don't know, *The Apprentice*. The "It Girl" was supposed to codesign a clothing line with a fashion designer, model it pageant-style on stage, create a successful business from it, and then some. And the promised prizes were incredible: a quarter of a million dollars in cash, the cover of *Vanity Fair*, a fully funded clothing line of my imagining, and a diamond tiara — yes — a diamond tiara that I was thinking of pawning for a new car. Altogether, this wasn't a bad deal.

After the cattle call, the producer combed through my modeling portfolio, the book I had published when I was in college, and a portfolio full of paintings that I also carried around with me back then. He looked at me like a prized cow. "Can I be honest with you? I think you're gonna win this thing." He leaned forward in closing. "If you sign up today, I will waive the fees and you just show up being you. Hell, I could probably fix it! Just say yes."

The pit of my stomach dropped. I've been told if something seems too good to be true, it usually is. Especially if someone is offering to unfairly cheat in order to make me the winner... there was definitely a trade there. Still, the sheer chaos of what this show was comprised of, more than any promise from a producer, made me feel warm and fuzzy knowing that I could pull this off. In chaos is where unique paths appear. I told him that I would compete, no freebies, and signed then and there.

As summer sweltered in the city of Los Angeles, filming began; and it was frenetic. Whether we were atmosphere modeling at a boutique on Melrose or getting our eyebrows plucked by the incredible Anastasia of Beverly Hills, the cameras were always rolling. We didn't exactly know what we were supposed to be doing. There was no clear path to winning; my only course of action was to keep it classy and use my ten years of modeling and acting experience. I had to deliver what I imagined an "It Girl" to be and bring all of my life along with me.

When I stood before the three judges in the heat of my final assessment, I gave them every bit of myself that I could in five minutes. Without knowing it, I was building my dream brand right in front of them. "I want all of my passion and creative drive to leave an influence for something better, bigger than myself. If I'm working with fashion, then it will be in a way that causes the least harm to people; it will be in a way that causes the least harm to the environment; and I'm dedicated to making this the new normal with all of my power." This was ages before the eco fashion movement became popular, so what I had to offer was new, honest, and spirited.

I didn't know it at the time, but that moment completely altered my journey as an artist. It opened up the doorway to more questions than answers, as I knew nothing about sustainability in fashion at the time. That night, as they announced me the winner of *America's It Girl*, I knew that the course of my life was now forever changed. My mission, from that moment on, was to understand sustainability, to understand the mind and why we crave consumption, and to create a new paradigm where we can have creative freedom to express ourselves with our clothes and do it with integrity. I was elated.

The director of the show was not interested in how I moved forward after the finale. So the business partner I was paired with and I started to ask ourselves the deeper questions about sustainability. Is it a waste product like fish skins? Could we make an entire line out of fish leather? Is it all hemp? What makes a product ethical? What is there to work with? Most importantly, what is the mindset of sustainability, and is it even possible in a system designed to always drive someone to buy more?

All of a sudden, what seemed like an innocent inquiry became an obsession. I woke up every day with that question on my mind. At that time, however, the internet did not have a lot to say; nor did the scientific community. I started sending direct messages on social media to activists, politicians, and third-party certification groups. I just wanted to make sure I was doing it right.

In many ways, I am grateful to have come up in the movement before everything was at your fingertips. Doing the research was like preparing a college thesis. Overnight I found a purpose that had no end in sight. *Has* no end in sight. Even as I put together interviews and follow the news today, we still don't know the full extent of the epidemic of fashion waste or plastic waste. The challenge of creating and designing with only the cleanest products available is paramount.

However, as I was putting together a draft of the first capsule collection — hand-drawn, with fabrics selected based on their sustainability — all communication from the *America's It Girl* production team went silent. Phone calls went straight to voicemail. Emails were not returned. Feelings of dread swept over my body as I went to bed at night thinking, "I should've known better." Finally, I heard from the producers and they told me they were filing for bankruptcy, and the only prize they could give me was a free associate's degree from an online school.

I was devastated. I had thought that this reality TV show would change my life. It might sound silly, but I was hoping for a direct path — something easy for once. I had been promised money in my pocket and all questions taken out of the equation. Instead, I was given a prize that was useless to me since I already had a bachelor's degree, and I was left with a burning desire to carry out the grand and energizing plan to change the world with sustainable fashion. Without their help, I was starting from the bottom.

Still, I held on to that crystal vision of combining activism, art, storytelling, education, and design. I moved forward into the world of eco fashion without any backing. The creative drive to tell the story of eco fashion became an award-winning fashion film, a children's book, a lecture series, and — yes — my clothing line, Holding Court. And now I have gathered everything I have learned into one beautiful place.

This book is a roadmap of everything I have learned since that time, and what has helped me develop the confidence to know I can overcome my need for material excess. The practices I have created will help you too.

Introducing Anthropocene

In each chapter ahead I share my story with you and how it led me to become an advocate for sustainable fashion. Additionally, I share stories from the activists, scientists, and policymakers who are changing the world for the better, one study at a time. I couldn't do this without them.

This book will get personal. We will approach ReFashioning as a mindfulness practice. We must learn to recognize the unconscious messages promoting fast fashion that we all encounter every day from advertising and peer pressure. The goal is to set you solidly within control of what clothes you buy and why. This is deep work, and I can't wait for you to discover what else might change within you as you explore your inner world.

Along the way, you will take inventory of your own buying habits with quizzes and questionnaires, look into what types of clothes you own, learn the yearly carbon footprint of your closet, explore how buying better can actually make you happier, and eventually do a highly guided closet purge and commit to a new way of buying in the future. With enough information, you will want to become an eco fashion warrior as well.

Just as we all have a life full of past experiences, so does Mother Earth. Earth is the cradle of life, the womb from which every plant and animal is generated, and she is the ultimate boss of our situation here. She is many millennia old, and she is extraordinarily unique. As the only place in the known universe to contain life, she has suffered at least five mass extinctions so far, where 90% of life forms disappeared forever.

Each of these mass extinctions was caused by either a cataclysmic event such as the Chicxulub comet which killed the dinosaurs 66 million years ago, or volcanic activity, massive fires — mostly some Earth-related catastrophe. After every disaster, Earth remakes her life-forms to become smarter, more efficient, and more self-aware. It is as if she is becoming more intelligent with age. She is growing up and reimaging herself into a stronger, more resilient being.

As Earth matured, she entered the age of Anthropocene, the age of humans. For all we know, Earth may not even be a teenager yet. She may just be in the beginning stages of self-awareness and self-discovery, still in the playground. Here we all are, just a cellular structure in her developing brain, a leap in consciousness, a new way to know oneself. We are only a small part of the whole.

Looking back on the early days of human existence, we know that clothing has always been a necessity. We barely have fur to speak of, and some of us traveled as far north as Siberia to make a home. In the beginning, the clothing we wore was often a byproduct of the animals we hunted. Imagine how many coats you could make from a mastodon. And as we began to learn to weave (cotton, silk, or linen), all the materials were sourced close by. We didn't have a mass trade network for ready-to-wear clothing. A hundred and fifty years ago, if your great-grandparents wanted a *new* dress or pair of trousers, someone in their community would make it from scratch specifically *for them*. The fact is, none of this is true anymore.

Since the spark of human self-awareness, we have experienced many shifts in our relationship with Mother Earth. What was once a symbiotic experience of growth and maturity has become unbalanced and toxic. The industrial revolution led to the creation of more apparel than we could ever wear, even with 8 billion people. We are now at a tipping point, and the Earth is preparing to shed us naturally and quickly. Humankind is accelerating this process by ignoring the glaring warning signs that Earth offers us.

Here are a few facts provided by the World Wildlife Fund for Nature in their *Living Planet Report 2022*:

- Wildlife populations have plummeted by 69% since 1970.
- Every day we lose 27 football fields' worth of wild forests — the lungs of the planet.
- 20% of the Amazon rainforest has disappeared in the last 50 years.
- Ocean acidification is occurring at a rate not seen in at least 300 million years, and the Earth is estimated to have lost 50% of its shallow water coral reefs in the last 30 years.
- Humans are responsible for releasing 100 billion tonnes of carbon into the Earth's system every ten years.
- Only 25% of land on Earth is substantively free of the impacts of human activities. This is projected to decline to just 10% by 2050.

So what happened? How did we go from living in symbiosis to becoming the catalyst for the next climate catastrophe?

I look at how the world is unfolding around us. Democracy is failing. Religions of the past are losing membership at record rates. Our global monetary system is backed by nothing but an idea. The systems that were created based on centuries of colonization and patriarchal ideas are broken.

I know what it is to be broken. Even as I write this book, moving from one country to the next — Portugal, Romania, Mexico, the United States — I am doing what I do when I do not feel whole. I am throwing myself into the unknown and avoiding the familiar so that I don't have to be in pain. The circumstances of brokenness change, but the ripple effect that broken people have on their environment is strong. And the result is chaos.

Broken people lose touch with the subtle; they lose touch with accountability; they lose touch with themselves. Ultimately, they lose their higher selves. This is where we are with our systems and where we are as people — living out the long-gone dreams of these broken systems.

I cannot tell you what kind of system needs to come next; that is not my pursuit. But I *will* say that if there is one thing I've learned, it is that we all need to move more into the stance of "the witness." We must adapt to Earth's needs and adjust our mindset to one that nourishes the whole, or she will leave us behind in the next phase of evolution. She will ditch us like yesterday's wisdom teeth.

That means we need to examine exactly what is causing the imbalance. The fashion industry is largely considered the second most polluting industry in the world. When you count how many trades are incorporated into it, you will find that it is not only toxic to the planet, but it can also be toxic to a person's self-image. This is why the Threefold Path is so important. The Threefold Path of ReFashioning is to bring into balance what you give, what you take, and the story you tell; and center it on sustainably maintaining itself as an unbroken triangle. Fashion is a key part of how we form our identities. Aside from our genetic makeup, how we present to the world in what we wear is a quick signal to others about who we are.

The issue lies in how we manufacture and throw away our clothes. We are creating a global identity that reinforces triviality. No one wants to be known as being cheap, but that is the reality of fast fashion.

So! This is where the real work begins. No one ever claimed that change is easy; but it can be fun, and it will be enlightening. Over the next few weeks you will devote time to introspection, to outward exploration, to letting go, and to clothing yourself in your new identity as a steward of the Earth.

To ReFashion is to transform your personal style into a conscious lifestyle — starting with your wardrobe. The process begs you to look deeply into the motives behind your buying habits and how you maintain the life cycle of your apparel. With the aid of questionnaires, tallies, experiences, interviews, and meditations, you will walk out of this experience with a whole new image.

The goal of ReFashioning is to create a clean slate so that you can step into your role as a steward of the Earth. This is huge! Given what we know thus far, we are inextricably tied to the welfare of the planet; and how we treat ourselves is reflected in how we treat the world around us. We have to heal ourselves to heal the planet, and a part of that is accomplished by finding out how our relationship to our self-image fuels our habits of consumption.

For this portion of the book, I recommend preparing a few things before you begin:

- A blank journal
- Access to a smartphone or computer with internet
- An accountability partner
- A willingness to let go
- Curiosity for who you will become

Breathwork

Mindfulness starts with the breath. With every inhale and exhale we have the opportunity to center ourselves and create confidence and inner peace. I am going to teach you a form of breathwork that unites dualities — two aspects that are in opposition, yet connected. This breathwork practice is rooted in Samkhya philosophy: in the unification of the female spark of Prakriti and the male witness of Purusha, but applied to aspects of the Threefold Path.

It is important to note here that the male energy of Samkhya rests on the right side of the body and the female energy on the left. With every breath you have the opportunity to blend them together. Imagine them as a double helix, intertwining and rising from the base of your spine to the crown of your head. Give each their equal place.

We will use this same principle for the aspects of *give* and *take* from the Threefold Path, placing *give* in the left side of the body with the Prakriti spark and *take* on the right side of the body with Purusha witness. This practice will help you find a beautiful balance within your own body to unite your masculine/feminine and bond together what you give/take from this planet in equal parts.

The goal is to infuse a state of sustainability (of one aspect feeding the other in complete symbiosis) within your physical body. We will revisit this practice several times until you begin to remember the balance of give/take as easily as drawing breath.

Find a comfortable place to sit. Straighten your back and relax your neck. Imagine a pair of lights resting in your pelvic floor, and breathe into them as *Prakriti give (left side)* and *Purusha take (right side)*. Begin to pull them up as ropes with every exhale, still attached to the base, and begin to twist them with every deep inhale. Inhale twist, exhale lengthen. Do this with patience and long deep breaths: visiting your sex organs, your solar plexus, and your heart. Let it intertwine inside at the throat, twist behind your eyes at the pineal gland (the control center of the body), and, with a deep exhale, let it exit your body through the crown.

Keep in your mind the image of the spark and the space for the spark to exist — the activator and part of yourself that manifests itself in action — the giver. And also the space that receives and takes information from the world using your senses — the taker. They exist together and can be harmonized as you breathe deeply.

It may take several times for the experience to feel balanced. Each time you reach your crown chakra, and it feels anything but good, send it away from you. As many times as it takes. Eventually you will have a cycle of breaths that spiral to the top with perfect balance.

When you reach the ecstatic feeling of inner balance at the top of your head, send your exhale back down your body and back into the seven chakra centers at your crown, your forehead, your throat, your heart, your belly, your gut, and your root. Nourish them in that beautiful feeling of wholeness.

Let's help create balance for Mother Earth by creating harmony within ourselves as we dance across her surface, giving and receiving in equal parts.

Community

In all things, it is easier to form new habits when surrounded by a community of peers who are committed to the same goals. When you are exposed to a group of people with the same lessons and experience in their minds, it reinforces the information within your own. ReFashioning is a fairly new concept, and I can imagine it being a challenge to find a peer group on your own, so I made it easy for you.

The link below takes you to a private online classroom where you can discuss your progress with other brave souls charting their path towards a sustainable wardrobe. Each questionnaire and tally within the book is available online and is there to help you keep a digital log of your personal habits, as well as give the team at *Environmental Style Now* real-world data on our life-cycle habits.

This platform provides easy access to all the links you will need throughout the workbook:

refashionworkshop.com

Go ahead and introduce yourself in the "Welcome" page of the classroom forum, and familiarize yourself with the layout of the page. Let your curiosity take you to read other people's experiences, and let it be an encouragement to you as you begin your own. In many ways the dialogue that happens there is just as important as the lesson. Hearing about someone else's worldview can help awaken ideas within yourself that you never imagined. And your ideas just may inspire other folks as well.

So, don't be shy! Share what's on your mind!

Now that you know where to find each other, it is a good time to decide who will be your accountability partner. You will want to choose someone who is active in your life, who knows you fairly well, and who can attest to the changes you make as you go further into the program. Aside from having someone to talk to about the process, your accountability partner will hold you to the commitments you are making with curiosity and support.

Intention Setting

1. Make a statement of intention in your journal and in the online forum. What would you like to gain from this experience? State your name before you write what you are committing to (e.g. "I, Courtney, would like to discover a new personal style that is in alignment with my actions to care for the planet. ReFashioning is going to heal me, Courtney, of my habit of buying fast fashion to look good on the internet.").

Revisit this statement when you wake up each morning. Write it at the top of your journal so that it is easy to find. By reading it every day, you will remind yourself of the change you wish to make.

2. Write down the name of your accountability partner and share with them your intention statement. Let them know that you are doing the ReFashion Workshop and will be reaching out regularly to share what you have learned and what you are doing.

3. By looking at the Earth as merely a backdrop for the drama of our lives, we ignore the sacred mystery that animates our body and soul, ultimately connecting us with the universe at an incomprehensible level. Our bodies alone regenerate themselves on a constant basis. Our stomach linings recycle every five days, our raw DNA every six weeks, and our skeletons every three months to ten years, leading us to regenerate an entirely new body every seven to ten years.

And while that is happening, the very atoms of your body sync up with random particles in the environment. Though separated by physical distance, quantum entanglement ensures that on a very basic level, no part of this universe operates completely independently. All atoms move as if two are one, completely in the same vibration and rhythm with the objects and entities around us, though sometimes separated by vast distances.

You are constantly regenerating along with the universe, as one! Totally entangled!

Consider your everyday activities, such as choosing what you are going to wear. First thing in the morning, you may tend to think of yourself in only singular terms.

Today, choose a mundane activity to explore your interconnectedness on an atomic level. Feel the sun when you take your dog on a walk and think, "I am one with the sun's rays." When you take off your shoes at the end of the day and go to put them away, consider how it took a global community to source the materials, sew, glue, and ship these shoes to you. Some of those entangled atoms are still in Bangladesh, connecting you right now to something unseen.

Write down your experiences in your journal at the end of the day.

4. A total ReFashioning requires a dramatic paradigm shift in how we view ourselves. You will have breakthrough moments as we move through the information. Think back to a time when you committed to great change for your personal well-being and then carried out the necessary actions to achieve fulfillment. Write down what that change was, and remember what it took to pull that off: strength in the face of opposition, breaking shared habits with loved ones, finding the limits of your self-discipline, and then pushing even further.

Write it all down so that you remember that you have done this before, and you will do it again.

5. As you proceed through the practices in each chapter, you will discover new levels of interconnectedness with people and the planet through experiences, reflection, and meditation. In this way, we will heal our relationship with ourselves and ultimately heal our relationship with the planet. Try to remember a time from childhood, or a time in meditation or prayer, when you felt an unwavering transcendent oneness with all that is — where you felt like your joy, peace, and understanding was as much inside you as outside you.

Close your eyes and reconnect with that feeling.

2

Buying Better

The consumer is actually responsible for a large part of the environmental impact of the clothing. Whether it's how long they wash it, or how long they wear it, or what happens to it when they're done with it.

— Tara St. James, Fashion Institute of Technology

What I am going to ask you to do in this chapter is not hard or complicated, but changing your mind is where the work comes in. I've had more access to more cheap clothing in the length of my career than you could imagine. If I can do this, you can do it too. As we move along in the book, we will go into detail about dyes, emissions, foreign ties, toxicity for people and animals, the oceans, and multinationalism. We will approach each with a magnifying glass. We've talked a little bit about the overall effects of humanity's presence on Earth, but now I'd like to get more specific about how your fashion-buying habits affect Mother Earth and her people.

Here are a few facts about fast fashion to consider, sourced from the United Nations Zero Waste #ActNow Fashion Challenge:

- The apparel industry consumes more energy than the aviation and shipping industry combined, accounting for 10% of the global carbon emissions.
- The fashion industry produces 20% of wastewater.
- $500 billion of value is lost every year due to clothing underutilization and lack of recycling.

If you're overwhelmed and don't know where or how to start, here are a few simple actions to buy better fashion from a place of centeredness. This is a good page to earmark.

I use the acronym ASSIST, created by the amazing human Kasi Martin of Fairtrade USA. Assist the world by reexamining your wardrobe. "A" is [to look at what you] **al**ready have. "S" is **s**econdhand shop — so going to a vintage store, a thrift store, or using apps like Poshmark. The second "S" is for **s**wap! You can have a clothing exchange with your friends and community; you can make it an event. "I" is for **i**ndie, so if you buy new, get it local. The last "S" is for **s**ew — so mend something that you already have. And then "T" is **t**raditional. A traditional mass retail store like Target should be your last resort.

- **(A)** Already have
- **(S)** Secondhand shop
- **(S)** Swap
- **(I)** Indie
- **(S)** Sew
- **(T)** Traditional

"The industry is built on sales, consumerism and mass consumption," says Tara St. James, "and without a complete shift in consumer behavior, which we are seeing right now, there can't really be true sustainable change within the industry."

To take it a step further, I have a few more pieces of advice for buying better. And it has to do with your awareness.

Buy Better — Smart and Less

Open your closet. Take a look in and take measure. Most of us have an overwhelming number of repeating styles of clothing already. Just for the amount of money and time saved alone, consider buying less. This is very anti-American culture in some ways, but it will set you towards the path to clear your mind for more important things.

But if you must buy, ask yourself these things before you pull out your wallet or close out your cart:

- Do I need this, or is it more of the same?
- Am I really going to wear it? Is the fit right?
- How long will this last?
- Is the investment worth the money?
- Will it really make me happy?

Choose Ethical

It can be difficult to know if a company pays their workers a living wage. But it is important to avoid those who obviously don't. Red-flag companies are Romwe, Shein, and the slew of online retailers that have an insane variety of apparel at next-to-nothing costs. These manufacturers create over 40,000 items per year, only 10,000 of which reach stores. The rest end up in incinerators.

Check your tag and do your research. Buycott is a wonderful app that will scan the barcode on a garment and give the facts about where it is made. At the end of this book you will find an appendix with a list of ethical brands to explore at your leisure.

Shop Local

Chances are, if your clothes are made locally, the manufacturer will adhere to stricter business practices — especially if you live in Europe or the US. Locally sourced apparel sometimes creates an opportunity for you to visit the warehouse where they manufacture. For example, Reformation offers a monthly guided tour of their Los Angeles factory floor! Shopping locally also minimizes your carbon footprint by avoiding the energy output from international shipping.

Secondhand

There are no disadvantages in buying secondhand. You can find one-of-a-kind unique outfits to set you apart, often at a fair price. Always check for holes and stains, the correct fit, and try the buttons and zippers to make sure they work. These days you can even skip the thrift store and shop for secondhand items online with easy-to-navigate apps. You can even sell your old looks and make a little money!

Timeless

Choose items that will age like a fine wine. You want something you can pair easily with other outfits and that will still look good in ten years. Not sure? Take your time; there is no rush to buy.

Quality over Quantity

Some garments are expensive because they are quality made and will last much longer than any fast-fashion outfit you buy. Inspect the seams and the weight of the fabric, and get a feel for the overall craftsmanship. You don't want to end up like I did, with a drawer full of cheap shirts falling apart in all the wrong places.

With ASSIST in your back pocket as a roadmap to buying better fashion, the key to navigating the map is practicing mindfulness, which is, in some ways, practicing meditation. You might feel tempted to overlook this one because it actually makes people squirm. The resistance to "dropping in" to the subtle mind is outrageous, and you might suddenly prefer to sweep the floor or do your taxes instead of sitting with yourself, and I get it.

When I committed to master my inner quiet, I set every single roadblock in my path I could invent. First I only wanted to train with "real" yogis in the country of origin, so I found the Sivananda Ashram at the Neyyar Dam in Kerala, India, and carved out a month for this experience. At the time, to even get to this ashram, I had to fly into the tropical city of Kochi, which took me two full, sleepless days. Then I took an unairconditioned four-hour train ride to Trivandrum, and then hailed a questionable 1950s Ambassador-style taxi cab — with no glass in the windows or seat belts — for a swerving, bumpy ride into the jungle. By this point it was late at night, and I was holding on to the door handle for support and questioning my every choice to want to learn to meditate.

Meditation is a clearing of the mind that can be found in almost every culture, not just Eastern philosophies. It turns your mind away from wandering thoughts and focuses it on one thing. It also helps to train the mind to stay quiet during tasks that might otherwise create an inner dialogue. We are going to pursue meditation as one of our methods for ReFashioning, in part because it creates a calmness where you can truly see your inner world. Also, as you continue to practice meditation, your happiness should increase. It is a scientific fact. I want your journey toward being a better steward of the planet to be as enriching, rewarding, and happy as possible. Let's hit those pleasure centers and delve into how meditation does this.

There are people who are masters of the quiet mind, expert meditators who have over 10,000 hours of meditation under their belts. Professor Hedy Kober at Yale University took a look at their brains under an fMRI scanner to see how they fired. During meditation, she found the meditators to have a very quiet prefrontal cortex, which is the region of the brain most active when the mind is chattering away, but she also found that the minds of the meditators fired in other regions of the brain simultaneously, showing an overall super-connectedness that non-meditators do not show. Their gray matter was also more substantial. Following the same meditators into regular life, she tested them during regular activities and found their minds less in the "default network" here as well.

This is phenomenal. We have the ability to change our levels of happiness with mind control! You can train your mind to quiet down, increasing your closeness to your inner self and increasing your happiness at the same time! Starting from this chapter onward, we are adding meditation as one of the key practices to help you recondition your mind to ReFashion your life.

The more you practice meditation, the more awareness you tap into. Awareness is the state of being conscious. It is the ability to directly know and perceive, to feel, to be cognizant of the events happening around you at any given time. It has less to do with education, and more to do with the simple ability to drop all internal storylines and absorb the bigger picture of life right now, in this moment.

Open awareness naturally leads to a richer understanding of what is going on at the point in time that you occupy. If you can teach yourself to be more perceptive, the brain works overtime to find patterns and connections that you might have otherwise missed. These patterns inform you of the nature of reality — the dance between people and material things, the motives behind people's actions, the balance of nature and our relationship with it.

When you are fully aware:

- You can center yourself at will.
- You are familiar with a place of peace and silence inside yourself.
- You aren't divided against yourself by inner conflicts.
- You can transcend local disturbances and remain unaffected by them.

- You see the world from an expanded perspective.
- Your inner world is organized.

Strengthening your awareness through meditation is critical to ReFashioning, and not just so that you can find a pretty new brand to buy from. When you strengthen your ability to open your mind in the present moment, you will connect with the oneness of all things. Once you find your place in the oneness, you will desire to consume more sustainably. And as you work towards analyzing your patterns, the greater awareness you have been cultivating will provoke changes in the way you interact with acquiring and discarding material possessions.

Having deeper awareness has more benefits than just being an eco fashion warrior. It quickly becomes a superpower when dealing with decision-making or conflict. You will see more of what is happening around you, and it offers more space for you to absorb the beauty of being alive.

There are many paths that lead towards deepening your connection with awareness. Practices that are centuries old inform just about every tradition. The sad reality is that for the past several decades, the developed world has tipped the scales out of balance. We live in a materialistic society. It is socially acceptable to have a pair of shoes in every color but never give back to your community by cleaning up trash or volunteering your time. When your "taking" becomes toxic, so does your "giving."

To create a new relationship with fashion, you must indulge in the awareness of the balance between giving and taking from the environment and from the other people on the planet. Identify what is healthy and what is toxic.

Our actions of the past were rooted in the desire to fit in, the fear of missing out, doubt, insecurity, and anger; and it can be easy to fall into these old patterns and habits sometimes. Living in a state of negative conditioning has its own flavor of awareness — one that is lower in vibrancy because it doesn't contribute to your happiness or the well-being of the planet at large.

Within everyone there is an awareness that isn't conditioned, that instinctively dances between the balance of giving and taking without overindulging. There are three ways to break down old conditioning, and their power increases in this order:

- Reflection — looking into old beliefs, assumptions and habits
- Contemplation — focusing on a thought until it expands into its fullness
- Meditation — sitting in silence or with a repetitive mantra until you move into the mind that isn't conditioned

Journal

1. Reflect: Write down five instances where your unawareness caused you to give of yourself in an unhealthy way. Maybe you gave an opinion that wasn't helpful to a friend. Perhaps you gave yourself too soon to someone you crushed on. It could be that you gave the city all of your trash and recyclables in one bin. Now consider five moments when you practiced unawareness in giving with your fashion habits. For example, you gave your friend a link to a website that sells fast fashion.

Now reflect on five times when you "took" or absorbed something from the world that was unhealthy for your mind, body, and spirit. You binge-watched something that made you feel ill. Or you ate a ton of junk food. And then consider five times you were unaware of "taking" with your fashion habits, such as impulse buying or buying fabrics that could shed a ton of polyester.

Reflect on five times your personal story took a nosedive (e.g. "I'm too fat" or "No one in the office respects me"). Now think of five personal stories you have told yourself about your relationship with fashion that were tied to anger, ego, insecurity, or similar negative emotions (e.g. "I will only fit in if I wear _____" or "I'm going to get the man I want by being sexier than other women" or "He hates it when I wear this, so I am going to do it out of spite").

2. Contemplate: Focus on each aspect of total awareness: giving, taking, and telling stories. One at a time, sit in silence with each attribute, and let the fullness of its meaning sink in. Write down your thoughts about it.

   Give ...
   Take ...
   Story ...

3. Meditate: Practice the following Meditation on the Heart for ten minutes as an exercise to contact that silent awareness within.

Find a place where you won't be disturbed. Sit quietly with your legs in the lotus pose, and your eyes closed, and rest your attention on your heart. As you breathe in and out, try to keep your attention there, right at the center of your chest. Feel its sensations arise and pass. If your attention wanders, bring it back to the heart and rest there.

4. ASSIST Practice: Look over the ASSIST outline one more time. Take into consideration anytime you have done one of the practices listed. Go down memory lane and remember how good it felt as a way of gaining new possessions in your life. Owning things isn't bad, but

how you get them says everything about your intention. If your intention is to be a steward of the planet, let's use ASSIST every time we shop. I do, and it is easier than you would ever imagine.

3

Certifications

Who gets to say what is sustainable? Who are the gatekeepers? If you have asked yourself these questions, then this is the chapter you've been waiting for. This was the particularly harrowing line of questioning that had me hooked after winning *America's It Girl*.

Filming had wrapped, the finale with Women's Entertainment Network was being edited, and my partner on the show and I were discussing the kind of clothing brand we would like to create as our winning prize. Would it be a luxury brand? Would we make ready-to-wear clothes? My background was in modeling and hers in designer handbags, but we had been given the opportunity to create a capsule collection that could be anything that we imagined.

We got to work. In my lifestyle I was already committed to some of the clean, hippie trends like eating organic, buying natural makeup, recycling, and sourcing as much as I could secondhand — from furniture to my wardrobe. But besides thrifting, I hadn't thought any further about the world of fashion manufacturing. Even as a model, the act of modeling had been more of a performance to me than a connection with the material. Honestly, one of the best things about shapeshifting as a model is that you get to return the costume and become yourself again at the end of the day.

But what did I want to do now that I had a new project steeped in the material world? I wanted to give it every bit of care I gave my dinner every night: know every ingredient, how it was grown, and what farmers' market it came from. The research began with the simple question: How do I make a clean clothing brand? And oh my! This was in 2014, before there were millions of articles on what I came to know as "fast fashion." The words that kept popping up were "sustainable," "ethical," and "zero waste." But this only scratches the surface of what can be certified as clean fashion.

Let's look at the definition of sustainability published in 1987 by the UN's former World Commission on Environment and Development, chaired by Gro Harlem Brundtland. And then we're going to review a few key ideas that the UN outlines in their *2030 Agenda for Sustainable Development*, published in 2015, and see where fashion fits into this worldview.

The Three Pillars of Sustainability

Sustainability is "the ability to continue a defined behavior indefinitely."

- **The Environmental Pillar:** Environmental sustainability is the rate of renewable resource harvest, pollution creation, and nonrenewable resource depletion that can be continued indefinitely. If they cannot be continued indefinitely, then they are not sustainable. This is the overall footprint from a business or industry, based on its carbon emissions, water usage, land reclamation, and waste.
- **The Social Pillar:** The general definition of social sustainability is the ability of a social system, such as a country, to function at a defined level of social well-being indefinitely. That level should be defined in relation to

the goal of their people and their ability to optimize quality of life for themselves and their descendants.

Now, "quality of life" is a much debated idea that differs wildly by culture, religion, class, and nation, so to define this universally is almost impossible. For that reason, this is the toughest pillar to nail down. But we can imagine that a system that prioritizes minimizing depletion of its society would also emphasize meeting basic human needs — such as a fair and living wage and the opportunity for higher education.

- **The Economic Pillar:** Economic sustainability is generally defined as the ability of an economy to support a defined level of economic production indefinitely. The ecological footprint is a measure of human demand on natural capital, that is, the quantity of nature it takes to support people and their economies. Total global capacity is estimated at 12 billion hectares (1 hectare = 10,000 square meters).

For a business to be economically sustainable, it must make a profit. That being said, profit cannot outdo the other two pillars. Key points of economic sustainability are proper governance, compliance, and risk management. With regard to governance, ideals must align with shareholders, community, and the consumer.

Here are the key goals of the United Nations Sustainable Development Agenda:

- **People:** We are determined to end poverty and hunger, in all their forms and dimensions, and to ensure that all human beings can fulfill their potential in dignity and equality and in a healthy environment.
- **Planet:** We are determined to protect the planet from degradation, including through sustainable consumption

and production, sustainably managing its natural resources and taking urgent action on climate change, so that it can support the needs of the present and future generations.

- **Prosperity:** We are determined to ensure that all human beings can enjoy prosperous and fulfilling lives and that economic, social and technological progress occurs in harmony with nature.
- **Peace:** We are determined to foster peaceful, just and inclusive societies which are free from fear and violence. There can be no sustainable development without peace and no peace without sustainable development.
- **Partnership:** We are determined to mobilize the means required to implement this Agenda through a revitalized Global Partnership for Sustainable Development, based on a spirit of strengthened global solidarity, focused in particular on the needs of the poorest and most vulnerable and with the participation of all countries, all stakeholders and all people.

Wow, we have a lot to do as a global community to reach the goal of being indefinitely sustainable across the board. All of these themes are interlinked and must be realized together to truly have a sustainable world system. But how does fashion fit into this puzzle?

The fashion industry touches countless other systems in the world. We have to look at agriculture, livestock, processing plants, dyes and chemical components, transportation, the workforce, employees, shareholders, corporate office waste, washing and drying, dry cleaning, waste processing, landfills, emissions, and toxic pollution. Hitting a sustainability goal in just *one* of these sectors would be a miracle.

Do you see the need for sustainability in fashion yet?

To make an impact here, we need a level of mindfulness that touches every level of the life cycle of your clothes. It may sound like a tall order, but this is where seeking out eco-certified brands helps cut down that time. You don't have to do them all at once, but let's explore what types of certifications exist today.

Here is an easy go-to list that often shows up on hangtags and labels. Any brands that have one of these certifications is already a step ahead of the rest. Take a look at what each one represents and protects, and follow up by researching their website.

- **Global Organic Textile Standard**
This is one of the most trusted certifications out there. Ninety-five percent of the fabric must be organic, and they check your supply line from soil to packaging: www.global-standard.org/

- **Oeko-Tex**
Fabrics must no longer be hazardous to health. This includes both natural and synthetic fibers. Oeko-Tex monitors the toxicity of the fabrics themselves on the factory floor. This will help ease the mind that you aren't wearing something bad for your body: www.oeko-tex.com

- **Made-by**
A nonprofit that develops tools for companies to produce more sustainably and monitors the ethical responsibility of manufacturers to have safe working conditions for garment workers: www.made-by.org

- **E.U. Ecolabel**
This is an environmentally conscious certification. They check for water usage, toxicology, and working conditions in European brands: www.ecolabel.net

- **Fair Wear Foundation**
This is a third-party organization that monitors the treatment of workers. It allows workers to report complaints and offers ethics

training for local-level factories to make sure they put laborers' needs above their profits: www.fairwear.org

- **World Fair Trade Organization (WFTO)**

This organization focuses on enterprises that impact 1 million livelihoods, 74% of whom are women. These enterprises transform local communities, pioneer upcycling, empower women, champion refugee rights, and practice organic farming. Their impact goes far and wide, and the WFTO is their global community: www.wfto.com

- **Fairtrade International**

Fairtrade focuses on the prosperity of farmers — from the working conditions to global price points. They will make sure the cotton, bamboo, tencel, and any organic fiber that is grown is sold with fair consideration for the cost of resources and labor that it takes to grow it: www.fairtrade.net

I met with Kasi Martin — longtime advocate of sustainable fashion and creator of *The Peahen*, a studio and fashion blog — over the phone during the first few months of the COVID-19 pandemic. She and I had already become online friends through the growing community of eco fashion advocates, but now she was celebrating her new position as head of marketing at Fairtrade USA. We talked about how her new job made an impression on the cause, and what she has learned along the way.

Exclusive Interview with Kasi Martin of Fairtrade

KM: "I got my start in eco fashion kind of in a roundabout way. In school, I studied two diametrically opposed things: the college of journalism and communications — pursuing that because I had multiple interests. But I was specializing in fashion on the side — by working at boutiques and internships in the fashion industry, working at a local fashion week when I was in Florida, and moving to Milan to study abroad in fashion journalism. I was based in the world of luxury fashion, and that's what I was attracted to. But then at the same time, I was doing a minor in sustainability and human rights in a program that was called Social Change Communications — how you rally people around change, change that is important to the world and protects the globe and is sustainable. And when I say sustainable I don't just mean environmental. I mean sustainable livelihoods that protect and ensure human life.

"When I graduated, I went to work for a PR firm in New York City. And that is where I had my 'aha moment' of, 'This is not the kind of industry I want to dedicate my time or talent to.' And that was one personal instance where I didn't see myself working my way up in that field on a basis of talent. It was very grueling and underpaid.

"But then there was a day when I had a life-altering experience with one of our accountants for Christopher Cain. Cain, he's a couture designer who's famous for these jelly dresses. If you look them up they are very nineties style. You can touch them and they have liquid inside. They're amazing. But one of them burst in the mail, and it was a couture gown upwards of $20,000. I remember the director of the firm getting very angry. And the whole situation made me think, 'What is this garment made of?' And then it led me down the rabbit hole of all the plastics things are made from petrochemicals. So I'm learning about sustainability and working in this industry, and it slapped me in the face: 'Wow, this is an incredibly unsustainable industry.' No one had started calling it out on the topic of fast fashion. I think when we look at millennials we are kind of the first offenders of fast fashion because we started consuming it. But then we were against it when we found out how egregious it was.

"So, anyway, I worked for a while with that firm and then moved back home and took a general marketing job. And that's when I said, 'What can I help do to change the fashion industry?' I decided to found my site, *The Peahen*. This was probably 2014 when I started it, and I started writing investigative pieces on things like 'Is Anthropologie Ethical?', 'Is This Brand Ethical?', 'What's the Difference between Artisan Made and Fair Trade?' It led me into a world of ethics where I could fuse my journalism background with reporting and try to help change the industry.

"As the years evolved, my business morphed into multiple things. As I was writing, brand collaborations started to happen. I moved my business to Austin, Texas, which is a city that has an appetite and affinity for sustainable living. Not so much sustainable fashion. But we were kind of a massive market for indie design and there was a lot of promise here, so when I moved here it led to more speaking opportunities to really bring that passion out; and I got passionate about consulting one on one with people and working with people to hone in their wardrobe. And that led to styling. So I was styling for magazines, I was taking people on tours of Austin of the ethical and independent brands that were around here, and teaching them how to build a more sustainable wardrobe. Curating vintage, really touching on every facet of sustainable fashion. And I loved it!

"That's how I morphed into this world. I had that business for six years, and then I wanted to join a bigger mission. I had never worked in the nonprofit space, and I thought that was my next phase as one of my goals — to be the head of PR for a firm that is either championing sustainable fashion or a nonprofit working in that space. And I happened to be speaking at a Fairtrade conference in Austin as an influencer ('How can Fairtrade brands and companies work with influencers?'). I was approached by someone at Fairtrade to do content writing, but I said, 'Actually I would like to work for you full-time.' And that's how that career shift happened. I moved out to the Bay Area for a while, and then eventually came back to Austin; and now I am more embedded in fashion supply chains.

"So, learning about Fairtrade factory standards, I am also super-embedded in other supply chains. We are famous for coffee and cocoa — they are our core products; but we have hundreds of thousands of products in our portfolio. Everything from quinoa, to baking supplies, projectiles... I work every day and read a whole book (about our products). It is incredibly challenging and exciting to be a part of Fairtrade."

CB: "What standards does Fairtrade practice?"
KM: "So how does it work? 'Fair trade' gets thrown around pretty loosely as a term. Someone can say, 'This was fairly traded,' but what does that really mean? There are three certification bodies in the world of fair trade. Which means, 'This was audited by a third-party standard.' Fairtrade USA is one of them. We have the majority of the market in the United States. Artisans and workers, farmers and fishermen are all over the globe, but we are more focused on the consumer market of the United States.

"When we say something is Fairtrade Certified, it means it has gone through a rigorous set of standards. For instance, for the agriculture industry there are over 200 compliances that a farm would have to go through to get certified. What is really cool about Fairtrade is, in addition to compliances and auditing we have community development funds. How that functions is, every brand that is paying into the Fairtrade system varies. For a bunch of mass retailers like Kroeger or Costco, they would pay additional money on top of whatever wage is provided for — on top of our standard — to these community funds. And they are different for every farm or factory. And they elect a body to use the funds.

"Say that there are 70% women at that farm; the elected body would have to be representative of that, and they vote on how to use the funds. Funds typically get used for everything, like building sanitation wells. In Mexico, they built a taqueria because the women, in order to work more, needed accessible food that they could take home. So they could pick up premade tacos on their way home. They are just using really inventive ways. Especially right now with COVID, our team is taking calls with the workers about how to take those premium dollars and make them more agile so that they can be used for medical supplies, or anything that would help the community stay safe and protected amid a massive pandemic."

CB: "Do you have any examples of what applies to fashion when it comes to compliance standards?"
KM: "We regulate everything from working hours to how long they're on the floor, health and safety hazards, chemicals. It depends on the factory and what is being produced. There are lines in there that ensure workers have access to bargaining and wages."

CB: "What do you think about the future of fashion?"
KM: "I am a data person, so I try not to be bleak. There are amazing things to be celebrated in this industry. I'm really keen on fashion technology and how that's being used. They aren't accessible to consumers now, but they will be in 20 years, and it's in collaboration with the big brands. There's a company called Bolt Threads, and they make a type of silk from spiders and they make leather from mushrooms. They launched into the market with a single brand partnership. It was in the MoMA with Stella McCartney, but that's how it just gets started."

CB: "Are there any facts about fast fashion that have surprised you along the way?"
KM: "I was absolutely stunned to learn that:

- Less than 1% of clothes get recycled. And that goes back to a system failure. People think that they might be donating to Goodwill or Salvation Army. But only 10% of those clothes are actually sold by charities; a lot are packaged away for profit and shipped away to countries like Pakistan or India, where they end up hurting their economy. Because they compete with locals who are selling clothes. We don't have the technology to properly recycle fabrics. They are more likely torn apart to be used as insulation for homes, but it eventually ends up in a landfill.

- It takes 14 bathtubs of water to make one cotton T-shirt. It is better than polyester in that it doesn't shed plastic microfibers, but it has a big environmental footprint when it comes to water. Especially if you aren't sourcing organic [cotton].
- Also that 152 million people are affected by child labor annually. That number has to come down. It has to.
- And just the fact that fashion is such a massive sector, and that's why creating change here is so important. It is the second largest economic activity in the world." www. fairtradeamerica.org

(Since the interview, Goodwill implemented a new sustainability initiative [See the Worth] where they intentionally design products using materials that could not be sold, remanufacturing them into new designs, and reselling them to fund their skills training program.)

The First Noble Truth of ReFashion: The Truth of Suffering

Kasi has a big heart for the suffering of people working in the garment industry, and I admire it greatly. All the certifying bodies I mentioned are working towards the same thing: to identify where human suffering is happening and to alleviate it with a standard set of rules that can be enforced.

Suffering happens to all of us at some point in our lives when we feel something has gone wrong. We feel sick from within, in pain and distress, and we cling to whatever we can to make ourselves feel better. At this moment, the truth is that all life on the planet is suffering.

Much like Siddhartha Gautama, the founder of Buddhism, taught centuries ago, you encounter Four Noble Truths along the path of awakening your inner connectedness with the planet. The Four Noble Truths are a conceptual framework for reaching a higher awareness of your unguarded need for sensation, which leads you to cling to impermanent things — like material possessions. And it provides a way out of the cycle.

The level of carbon dioxide is now higher than it has been in 3 million years, and fashion is estimated to be responsible for half our emissions in the next 20 years. We are only beginning to feel the impact. The blanket of carbon dioxide (CO_2) is being joined by enormous releases of methane gas from the melting of the permafrost. Methane is 86 times more volatile than CO_2. Every day, the release of carbon dioxide is 400,000 times that of the Hiroshima bomb.

With each degree of rising heat, agriculture fails, wild animals struggle to survive and go extinct, and the weather becomes more violent. Humans, being a life-form, also suffer along with all the rest of life on this planet. Suffering is an innate part of being alive on this rock, but it doesn't have to be that way. Not on the mass scale we see unfolding today.

Sadly, one species contributes the most to this suffering. You've got it, it's us. We have conquered the planet with infrastructure and industry, and fashion is considered the second most polluting industry in the world. We continue to set aside protective measures in order to increase the bottom line. So it's no surprise that humanity's unfettered desire to own things has become fuel for the suffering of all life-forms. We need to open our hearts to fully recognize the scale of our impact on the planet, the truth of the planet's suffering.

Journal

In your journal, answer the following prompts:

1. Reflect on a moment in your life when you saw an ecosystem — small or large — that was damaged by industry. Write down your personal experience. Where was it, and what was damaged? Have you ever experienced what it is like to be in an ecosystem destroyed by the fashion industry? Google it to see what it's like.

2. Now that you have a strong visual of a negatively impacted ecosystem, do a little research on exactly what it was that damaged it. Next to what you wrote down first, write down what caused it to decline, and contemplate on a time when you yourself used that product.

3. What is the product? Petroleum? Salt? Plastic? Contemplate the last time you used that product, and let yourself feel the connection between the suffering ecosystem and your purchase.

4. Meditation: Find a quiet place where you won't be disturbed for ten minutes. Sit in the lotus position if you can, and close your eyes. Let your breath guide you into a place of emptiness in the mind. If you feel a thought popping up, become aware of it, and let it slide back into nothingness. This is a mindfulness meditation to help you clear your mind for the exercise ahead. It is best to approach self-inquiry with an open mind.

Your buying habits directly touch upon your contribution to the state of the planet. They are an extension of your desire, your identity, and your creativity. Are you ready for a radical change in how you interact with consumption? Right now we are thinking broadly, but we are little by little closing in on your habits with fashion in particular. Before you can reinvent your established connection with the physical world, you need to see where you are right now.

Where Are You Right Now?

The following quiz will help you understand your history of purchasing apparel. You can write directly into the book, or record it in your journal.

Answer the following questions YES or NO:

YES __ NO __ I go out of my way to style myself from apparel made by local designers.

YES __ NO __ "Made in My Region" is important to me.

YES __ NO __ I tend to shop with a distinct style in mind.

YES __ NO __ My wardrobe is full of clothes that I wear frequently, without a lot of sidelined options.

YES __ NO __ I have bought additional products that help collect lint when I wash my laundry.

YES __ NO __ Most of my apparel is made from natural fibers.

YES __ NO __ I tend to keep the clothing I buy for several years.

YES __ NO __ I never throw away old clothes in the trash.

YES __ NO __ I have researched my favorite brands and know their brand policies.

YES __ NO __ I try to avoid knockoff designs from the runway.

YES __ NO __ I have contacted my favorite brands when I think they could do it better.

YES __ NO __ I own clothing made from natural dyes.

YES __ NO __ I am aware of my contribution to carbon dioxide pollution.

YES __ NO __ I have actively changed my apparel-buying habits in the past year.

YES __ NO __ I have looked into where my clothing is made.

YES __ NO __ I have had conversations with friends about fast fashion.

YES __ NO __ I know how much water it takes to make a pair of jeans.

YES __ NO __ I have seen *The True Cost*.

YES __ NO __ I have paid more for an item of clothing because I knew that the manufacturer paid the worker a fair wage.

YES __ NO __ I have been to a sewing house before.

YES __ NO __ I have dropped off clothes at a Salvation Army or Goodwill store.

YES __ NO __ I thrift shop.

YES __ NO __ Knowing that my choice of clean apparel makes a difference makes me feel good.

YES __ NO __ I am aware that my actions have a ripple effect that contributes to the whole of society.

TOTAL YES:____

Evaluating your score

0–10 Yes answers: You have decided on the majority of your style choices by pure convenience. Of course you have taste and a wardrobe that fits your personality, but you have not thought any further than that. If it is cute and easy, it is an easy choice for you. This is no fault of yours — the sustainable fashion movement is new, and there has never been more advertising for new clothes than there is right now!

Given the opportunity to broaden your awareness, you are willing to take a look. You have a lot to chew on. And you have the most work ahead.

10–20 Yes answers: You have read articles or seen the coming movement of clean fashion, and you have already dipped your toes in. Maybe you have friends who have committed to changing their fashion habits, and you are not skeptical about the information. But you're not completely convinced that there is an urgency to go all in.

You aren't yet aware of how your buying habits are one with your integrity. You haven't stepped into your role as a steward of the Earth.

20–25 Yes answers: You have made a conscious effort to shift away from the old paradigm. It wasn't easy, but the fruit of your choices is an ease of mind and spirit, as well as the knowledge that you are doing the best you can to be a mindful little Earthling. You are here because you know there is always more to learn, and for you to continue in your commitment, you should constantly feed that hunger.

You have embraced your role as a steward of the Earth, and are eager to be even better.

Take what you have learned about yourself and consider some of these questions the next time you want to buy an outfit for yourself. By the end of this book you will want to have moved up on the scale by at least one bracket. The more often you consider how your habits have formed, the easier it is to change them. You will be refashioned in no time at all.

4

Dyes

The dye industry was the birth of the pharmaceutical industry and the birth of the chemical industry. So if you really want to get meta on toxic chemicals, clothing was the start!
— Dr Sam Shay, researcher, author, and creator of "The 10 Pillars of Health"

In the dry, crackling heat at Burning Man — a monumental pop-up city that calls itself a festival but hosts 80,000 people for a week on a dry lake bed in Nevada, with workshops for everything you can imagine from psychedelic plant medicine to a Q&A with an astronaut — I spent my first few days under the welcome shade of a dome learning about the fascinating theory of biohacking. Biohacking is basically a twenty-first-century term for making incremental changes to your lifestyle and habits so that you can operate at your highest possible mental and physical capacity. At the end of his three-day seminar, I stopped to ask Dr Sam Shay, the instructor, if he had any awareness of how the fashion industry might be a stumbling block to biohacking. And he had a lot to say on the subject.

"The chemical industry actually started in Germany with the dye industry," he told me, hiding in the dusty shade of a covered dome. "You learn this in organic chemistry class. In 1856 there was an academic lab where a PhD student named William Henry Perkin was trying to mix a form of quinine for malaria treatments, whereas quinine was extracted from exotic trees and was very expensive. So he tried to take coal tar as a base, and it resulted in this nasty black goo.

"His professor made him clean it up, and the grad student used a white towel to mop up the substance; and even though it appeared black, when he mopped it up the white towel stained purple. This was the first time in history that someone made a synthetic dye, and it happened to be purple, which was the most coveted color in the world.

"Now, purple is a royal color. And the reason it's a royal color is because it was freaking difficult before the industrial revolution to dye things purple, because there's very few things in sufficient quantities to make things blue or purple. It was a royal color because it was so rare. Now, here comes this guy, who suddenly figured out how to synthetically make the color purple. And with fabric and design — pillowcases, carpets — everyone wanted purple. And so suddenly this massive exploitation happens in the chemical industry because they figured out how to make a color!"

The color purple was the catalyst that launched the chemical industrial complex, and in just 150 years we went from one synthetic chemical to over 350,000. Now, almost every piece of clothing in your home is colored with a synthetic dye. Why is that a problem, you ask? Because along the way, additives and fixatives were used to help colors bind to fibers, and these have been proven to be incredibly harmful to all life-forms. In fact, they are the biggest carcinogen in the entire country of Indonesia, according to Greenpeace.

Harmful Dyes and Chemical Additives according to Greenpeace's Detox Catwalk

- **Azo dyes:** These are used in dyeing textile fibers, particularly cotton, but also silk, wool, viscose, and synthetic fibers. They are considered easy to use, are relatively cheap, and provide clear, strong colors — they are most commonly found in vibrant reds, yellows, oranges, and browns. There are approximately 2,000 azo dyes on the market. The majority of azo dyes are water soluble and are therefore easy for the body to absorb, and this takes place through inhalation and swallowing of dust as well as through skin contact. Azo dyes are also toxic to aquatic organisms and cause long-term adverse effects in aquatic environments. There is a risk of exposure when wearing garments or accessories that contain azo dyes, or when sleeping in such bedclothes.
- **Alkylphenols:** Commonly used alkylphenol compounds include nonylphenols (NPs) and octylphenols, and their ethoxylates. Particularly, nonylphenol ethoxylates are used to create stability in synthetic dyes to give them a longer shelf life. NPs are widely used in the textiles industry in cleaning and dyeing processes. They are toxic to aquatic life, persist in the environment, and can accumulate in body tissue and biomagnify (increase in concentration through the food chain). Their similarity to natural estrogen hormones can disrupt sexual development in some organisms, most notably causing the feminization of fish.
- **Phthalates:** Phthalates are a group of chemicals most commonly used to soften PVC (the plastic polyvinyl chloride). In the textile industry they are used in artificial leather, rubber, and PVC, and in some dyes. There are substantial concerns about the toxicity of phthalates such

as DEHP (bis(2-ethylhexyl) phthalate), which is reprotoxic in mammals, as it can interfere with development of the testes in early life. The phthalates DEHP and DBP (dibutyl phthalate) are classed as "toxic to reproduction" in Europe and their use is restricted.

- **Chlorobenzenes:** Chlorobenzenes are persistent and bioaccumulative chemicals that have been used as solvents and biocides, in the manufacture of dyes, and as chemical intermediaries. They are used to help dyes bind to synthetic polyester. The effects of exposure depend on the type of chlorobenzene; however, they commonly affect the liver, thyroid, and central nervous system. Hexachlorobenzene (HCB), the most toxic and persistent chemical of this group, is also a hormone disruptor. Within the European Union (EU), pentachlorobenzene and HCB are classified as "priority hazardous substances" under regulations that require measures to be taken to eliminate their pollution of surface waters in Europe. They are also listed as "persistent organic pollutants" for global restriction under the Stockholm convention, and in line with this they are prohibited or scheduled for reduction and eventual elimination in Europe.
- **Heavy metals:** Cadmium, lead, mercury, and chromium(VI) have been used in certain dyes and pigments used for textiles. These metals can accumulate in the body over time and are highly toxic, with irreversible effects including damage to the nervous system (lead and mercury) or the kidneys (cadmium). Cadmium is also known to cause cancer. Uses of chromium(VI) include certain textile processes and leather tanning; it is highly toxic even at low concentrations, including to many aquatic organisms.

This list is not new news. For years I had been reading articles about toxicity in apparel (and trust me, the list is exponentially larger than this). But I wanted to know in real time just how bad it had become. Nothing can substitute for what you see with your own eyes. So I reached out to Greenpeace in Indonesia and coordinated a meeting with Adi Yadi, member of the organization Pawapeling and a representative on the Island of Java, to meet me at the site of the dirtiest river in the world — the Citarum River in the textile city of Bandung, Indonesia.

I met up with a cameraman, Adi, and an interpreter at midday on a bridge spanning the Citarum just outside the largest manufacturing plant in the district. With constant applications of bug spray, dodging mountains of trash and open waste ducts from the factory, we trekked along the snaking river, covering our noses to block a strange burn in the air. An absolute rainbow of colors was swirling into the water directly from a line of pipes protruding across the river from the Gistex factory. It could have been beautiful if my eyes weren't stinging. Adi stopped just in front of the building and we began a conversation.

"Gistex is a factory that produces liquid waste that contains hazardous chemicals, poisonous and dangerous," he started. "It is disposed of in the Citarum River. Citarum River is the longest river in West Java. It is a strategic place in West Java as well as nationally because it produces three power plants and it becomes a reservoir for 80% of people in Jakarta, the capital city of Indonesia.

"Gistex is one of the factories that from our investigation produces GAP and H&M, famous brands. Meanwhile, here, we can see that they aren't eco-friendly, and Gistex itself is one of thousands of factories that are located at Citarum River.

"Science shows that the properties of some of the most popular fabric dyes are carcinogenic when consumed and absorbed through the skin. That is a problem for us because we wear clothing every day, and for the people of Java it's a problem of survival, because waste from this industrial activity contains heavy metal that can be consumed and accumulated from water and food chains, and it causes cancer for babies and disturbs their growth hormonally. We already researched that textile liquid waste is dangerous because it contains chromium hexavalent, lead, copper, and other heavy chemicals. The chemicals are categorized as poisonous and dangerous waste."

He paused and looked past the rainbow-colored river, down the shoreline on our side of the bank. Just up the way was a building, if I could call it that — a house made of cinder block, tarp, branches, and all kinds of hodgepodge materials. "Let's go on a walk," he said.

A gaggle of chickens and barking dogs came running towards us and then away from us. Hanging from the trees were old CD-ROMs, artworks, and objects made with care, and suddenly there were more faces than I could have imagined coming out to meet us. An aged gentleman with the presence of the head of the household came to greet us, and after a few pleasantries he and Adi jumped into conversation.

"What is your hope for the Citarum River?" Adi asked.

"My hope is that the Citarum River becomes clean. Because Citarum used to be clean, the water can be used to wash yourself and clothes. Everyone you see here was bathed in there as a baby. Small fishes always come near my body when I swim but the fish are now gone."

"It's because of what?"

"It's because of the factory pollution."

"So the impact is very clear?"

"Yes. It can't be used to wash and bathe because it causes itch. Others are still affected by itch just by breathing and when we brush our teeth we have sores on our mouths. I have to carry water all the way from the city. See the colors like red, black, green, yellow. I have even lifted some corpses from Citarum. Moreover when the rainy season comes, there is so much waste we can walk on the waste surface."

We thanked the family, some 30 people, giving hugs and unspoken gratitude for their welcome. The gentleman showed us some of the objects he had pulled from the river. They ranged from refrigerators to cellphones. I've never felt so helpless in the face of hospitality. I wanted to give them a new house, give them comfort; but most of all I wanted that smokestack of a factory across the river gone from their lives.

In my heart I knew that what I bought on a whim on a Tuesday in California was the middle of a butterfly effect originating far away in some unimaginable place. But now I don't have to imagine. I have met some of the people affected by my frivolous choices, and they are suffering. And one thing I *can* control is what brands I buy from.

Your Favorite Brands

Most of us don't have the luxury of time — or interest for that matter — to sit at home and weave flax into linen to make a set of sheets for our beds. Any of our basic needs — food, shelter, and clothes — are now mass produced so that we can go on with our lives without having to think about tasks of survival like stockpiling lye to make homemade soap. In some ways, we can all be grateful that most of our needs have been developed for us. We have more time on our hands than any other generation to date. But breaking the direct connection from commodity to product has thrown us consumers into the dark. We have forgotten that our relationships with our products contribute to our personal impact on the environment.

No matter how humble a life you live, you have an impact on the environment. From an ecological standpoint, we are inseparable from the environment, with a dance of give-and-take at every moment. There are countless ways that we can take from the planet and give back to it, and when you choose to purchase products from a brand, their "taking" becomes your "taking." Their pollution becomes your pollution. Their crimes against humanity become yours.

You contribute to the cycle of give/take on whatever level the manufacturer has chosen. Are you in the know about your favorite brand's policies? Have you checked to see if they are transparent and fact-checked? Once you become aware of how deep your responsibility extends, knowing these answers is the next step. And then you get to decide if you can consciously stand by the brands you have historically supported.

Journal

1. Reflect on your favorite apparel brands whom you regularly shop from. This isn't an aspirational list; it is a list of actual name tags within your closet. Write down five names.

2. Contemplate your perceived idea of what their ethical and environmental policies are. Use your imagination, and in the space next to the list write down how you imagine this brand contributes to environmental sustainability, to economic sustainability, and to social sustainability.

3. Now, take a moment and close your eyes. You love wearing this brand and you want to continue feeling good about it. Imagine how you wish they would contribute to the UN Sustainability Goals: impact on people, planet, prosperity, and peace. Write down this aspiration as if you are sending a letter to a friend you are having an intervention with.

4. Meditation: For ten minutes, in a quiet place, close your eyes and sit in the lotus position, if possible. Use your breath to quiet your mind, following it in and out, as it enters your mouth and into your chest, and as it leaves. Let your breath calm your mind as you feel all aspects of your body. Do a body scan from toes to head, stopping with your breath if you feel pain or anxiety.

Lead your breath to those places, and sit in a moment of concentration with the pain and discomfort until it goes away. Doing this daily can help you discover places in your body where you hold stress, and can help you recover from it while you recondition your heart and mind to ReFashioning.

Exercise

The impact of your favorite fashion brand may be more negative than you know. Now is the point where you find out exactly what their relationship to sustainability is.

You will need your computer and your list from the last journal entry. On the web, and in an app, there is an amazing database right at your fingertips: Good On You is a sustainability watchdog, and they keep tabs on all the major brands, and many boutique brands. Their brand directory tracks each label's relationship with people, planet, and animals.

In the ReFashion Workshop online class, follow the link [Good On You].

1. Go ahead and enter your top five favorite brands into Good On You's "Brand Directory." Take a good look at how they are rated, and write down what the directory says about their impact on people, planet, and animals. Take a moment to let it sink in.

By buying from these brands, you walk in line with them. Your impact is directly tied to the practices they have committed to. Do you feel good about their level of commitment? Does it agree with you?

2. Remember that letter you wrote earlier in your journal? The letter to your favorite brands where you imagined

how great they could be? Now that you know exactly where they land in their relationships with sustainability, adapt the letter to target their weakest spots.

Think of it as an intervention. A friend needs to hear from you when they are way out of balance and harming themselves and others by negligence, and your favorite brands need to hear from their customers in the same manner. They depend on you to keep them in business, and if you really love what they make, it's on you to let them know that they can do it better.

3. Time for some action. Find the contact information for your top five favorite brands, and send them that letter! It can be through Instagram, Facebook, or the "contact" page of their website. Just make sure it gets to them. This is your letter of intervention, and an important step for you as you explore your desire to buy fashion that honors the UN Sustainability Goals. They may not respond to you, but you will know that eyes have seen it, and that is just as important.

5

Emissions

Emissions are an invisible killer, and this is one of the many reasons why climatologists struggled to convince the world of global warming in the 1990s.

What we call emissions are the negative side of our essential greenhouse gases. These gases, when in the perfect percentages, contain all the ingredients for life on Earth. It is the absence of greenhouses on Mars that would make it so challenging for us to move there. We need oxygen, nitrogen, and yes, carbon dioxide; don't forget that plants breathe carbon dioxide, and we absolutely could not live without plants, the lungs of the planet.

Once again, it is imbalance that creates our problems in life. We consider emissions to be manmade greenhouse gases that are a byproduct of industry. The danger lies in how much output there is compared to what the Earth can naturally recycle. Industry left unchecked has us releasing more carbon dioxide, methane, and nitrous oxide than the planet can recycle — all chemicals that trap heat within the atmosphere of the planet. Meanwhile we are cutting out the lungs of the world, our natural forests, that would otherwise reset our fragile ozone system.

This puts us in incredible danger of overheating our planet to the point of mass extinction. It is happening in waves, such as rising water levels due to melting glaciers. And changing weather patterns, due to new and chaotic mixing of hot and cold water in the oceans, which leads to massively destructive storms. And with the change of temperature, eventually our forests will collapse.

What no one is talking about is how one industry is the summation of several of the biggest offenders, making it quite the elephant in the room. I have already touched on just how many trades the fashion industry involves, and it is unbelievably expansive, but to begin to tell you its impact with emissions, I turn to the experts.

Doing his best to make light of the climate crisis, climate analyst Ethan Brown hosts a podcast on PBS, called *The Sweaty Penguin*, where crisis meets comedy, and he was kind enough to take a phone call with me.

"Yeah, so we did an episode on fast fashion," he began. "It was definitely really an eye-opener and one that stuck with me. But the fashion industry is responsible for 10% of global carbon emissions. At the pace at which people are buying more and more, the fashion industry's greenhouse gas emissions will surge more than 50% by 2030. In the US, it's outpacing the growth of every other major waste-stream category. Waste has its own emissions."

Let's look at what Our World in Data has to say about how much each industry that touches fashion contributes to emissions (which total 100%).

- **Transport (16.2%):** This includes a small amount of electricity (indirect emissions) as well as all direct emissions from burning fossil fuels to power transport activities. These figures do not include emissions from the manufacturing of motor vehicles or other transport equipment.

- **Energy use in commercial buildings (6.6%):** Energy-related emissions from the generation of electricity for lighting, appliances, and so on, and heating in commercial buildings such as offices, restaurants, and shops.
- **Fugitive emissions from oil and gas (3.9%):** Fugitive emissions occur when there is leakage of methane to the atmosphere during oil and gas extraction and transportation, often accidentally from damaged or poorly maintained pipes. This also includes flaring — the intentional burning of gas at oil facilities. Oil wells can release gases, including methane, during extraction; producers often don't have an existing network of pipelines to transport it, or it wouldn't make economic sense to provide the infrastructure needed to effectively capture and transport it. But under environmental regulations they need to deal with it somehow; intentionally burning it is often a cheap way to do so.
- **Chemicals and petrochemicals (2.2%):** Greenhouse gases can be produced as a byproduct from chemical processes; for example, CO_2 can be emitted during the production of ammonia, which is used for purifying water supplies, cleaning products, and as a refrigerant; and it is used in the production of many materials, including plastic, fertilizers, pesticides, and textiles. Chemical and petrochemical manufacturing also produces emissions from energy inputs.
- **Wastewater (1.3%):** Organic matter and residues from animals, plants, humans, and their waste products can collect in wastewater systems. When this organic matter decomposes, it produces methane and nitrous oxide.
- **Landfills (1.9%):** Landfills are often low-oxygen environments. In these environments, organic matter is converted to methane when it decomposes.

- **Agricultural soils (4.1%):** Nitrous oxide — a strong greenhouse gas — is produced when synthetic nitrogen fertilizers are applied to soils. This includes emissions from agricultural soils for all agricultural products, including food for direct human consumption, animal feed, biofuels, and other nonfood crops (such as tobacco and cotton).

- **Livestock and manure (5.8%):** Animals (mainly ruminants, such as cattle and sheep) produce greenhouse gases through a process called 'enteric fermentation' — when microbes in their digestive systems break down food, they produce methane as a byproduct. This means beef and lamb tend to have a high carbon footprint, and eating less meat is an effective way to reduce the emissions of your diet.

  Nitrous oxide and methane can be produced from the decomposition of animal manure under low oxygen conditions. This often occurs when large numbers of animals are managed in a confined area (such as dairy farms, beef feedlots, and swine and poultry farms), where manure is typically stored in large piles or disposed of in lagoons and other types of manure management systems. "Livestock" emissions here include direct emissions from livestock only.

Exclusive Interview with Climate Analyst and PBS Host Ethan Brown

EB: "*The Sweaty Penguin* is a comedy climate podcast I host. It is presented by PBS in the National Climate Initiative, 'Peril and Promise.' And we're trying to make climate change less overwhelming, less politicized, and more fun. So my background: I did a dual degree at Boston University in environmental analysis and policy, and film and television. And I think that, going back into high school, even when I first learned about climate change, it was just really overwhelming, really stressful. And it was hard to find it interesting because of that. And that's really why I ended up studying in college, kind of forcing myself at first because it just seems so important. But once I kind of took the time to learn about it, I realized that there were maybe better ways of communicating it to allow other people such as my younger self to be able to engage more easily. And that's kind of the inspiration for the podcast."

CB: "What about fast fashion in particular shocked you as an analyst?"
EB: "Fast fashion is possibly one of the most inefficient things I've seen, just to create a cheaper product at the time of purchase. Using lower-quality fabrics, you're creating much less sturdy products, and then you buy it cheap. But you wear it three times, run it through the wash, and it disintegrates, then you have to buy eight more of them. Whereas if you just had one quality shirt, you could probably end up saving money in the long run. That is a great example of how the environment and the economy — be it globally, or just our personal pocketbooks — are very often aligned. Recycled clothing is a big challenge, because a lot of clothes are made with a blend of fabrics. So it won't just be cotton, or just polyester. Might have both; it might have other stuff in there. And to recycle it, you have to be able to separate those things. And you can't easily do that. So that's definitely a challenge in terms of trying to create more of a closed-loop supply chain where you're not having to create new material all the time. The other issue that stuck out was with donating clothes. I think a lot of people feel like, by donating clothes, they get another life. But actually a lot of clothes don't get a second life; we were finding that a large portion of the clothes that are donated will get put on boats and delivered by the ton to countries in Africa who don't need that many clothes.

So there are places in Africa where they're just burning up piles, releasing more emissions into the atmosphere."

CB: "You approach the climate crisis with a humorous edge. I know you did an episode of *The Sweaty Penguin* on fast fashion. How did you approach that?"
EB: "One of my favorite things we did was make a video of a catwalk, and at the time our sound editor Frank Hernandez had done a voiceover where he was talking about the clothes, but instead of describing the design he said things like, 'Check out this denim jean jacket at 6000 gallons of water,' or 'This leather jacket only cost 24 kg of CO_2.' I thought it was such a fun video.

"There was a fast-fashion brand that recently put out a new line of clothing that had messages about climate change and sustainability on the shirts. Shirts that said 'Protect the Planet' and 'Listen to Your Mother' but they were all made of polyester and literally were fast fashion. Oh, my gosh, the irony. I can't... So great! I mean, in a bad way. Great and terrible."

CB: "What is one thing you would change in the fashion industry today if you could?"
EB: "Brands need to be transparent about their supply chain. It is one very simple thing that could be done, and I think it's either starting to happen or being discussed. I don't like advocating specific policies per se, but just to put an option on the table. You can basically tell brands that they have to be transparent about their supply chain, where everything came from, where it went through — all of that information — whether or not there was child labor, hopefully not. So you can require that they just give that information. That's a somewhat small step. That's something that the brands may not have, you need to go get. But what that does is just give the information to customers to allow them to make an informed decision.

And from the perspective of, like... even just talking from a capitalism perspective, that's a fundamental piece of how a free market is supposed to operate — is that consumers have full information about the products they're buying, so they can make an informed decision.

"If consumers don't have that information right now, then it's not a free market. While that even, it's like, it sounds like a regulation, but it's actually just trying to preserve the freedom for people to make their decisions, and at the same time, could have a major impact. Because these companies would have to figure out their supply chain, and then they'd have to, if there was child labor in it, I think they'd try to get rid of that pretty quickly if that information is going to be public. And then people can make better decisions. Obviously, you can get a lot more intense than that if you want to. You can say no child labor; you can say you need to do X,Y, Z with these fabrics, or you need to reduce emissions in this way. There are a number of ways you can go. But I think even that small baby step could be something that could make a big difference."

Practice: Track Your Emissions

How can we bring our emissions as a species back into balance? By taking stock of our personal impact. Have you ever analyzed how dirty your closet is? It is time to find out exactly how many pounds of CO_2 emissions you contribute each year to the environment.

Go online and take the quiz: ReFashion Workshop [Fashion Footprint Calculator].

Accountability

Call or text your accountability partner and tell them the results of your test. It is important to be honest and let them know how it made you feel. Disappointed? Affirmed? Suggest they take the test too so that you can compare.

Journal

1. Reflect on the results of your Fashion Footprint Calculator. How many pounds of CO_2 do you generate in a year? Write it down. How has this number surprised you? How do you think you compare to your friends and family?

2. Contemplate on what that number looks like in reality. Imagine it as a pile of coal or a gaseous cloud that is attached to you like a leash. It is a weight, a burden you bring with you. Imagine how good it would feel to have that imaginary cloud shrink substantially. Contemplate on the reality that it is within your power to do that.

3. Meditate: Choose a quiet place to spend the next ten minutes. Sit in the lotus position and close your eyes. Follow your breath in and out until it relaxes you, and you feel connected with yourself. Let your breath expand more and more, growing your chest in size and power. Feel your connection with the room. Listen actively to the rustle of the world outside of yourself without naming it, and let it be one with you. You are both separate and one with the physical world. Explore it with your breath.

6

Foreign Ties

*Globalization is a double-edged sword. It's like
licking honey off the razor's edge.*
— Carroll Dunham, *National Geographic* anthropologist
and cofounder of Around the World in 80 Fabrics

While traveling through Asia in my late twenties, I visited
the far-flung archipelago of Raja Ampat. This South Pacific
paradise is a chain of pointed limestone islands, dotted with
lush jungle, surrounded by a crystal blue marine ecosystem with
the healthiest remaining coral reef on the planet. But it wasn't
just the untouched nature that touched my heart; it was the
uncomplicated way that the Indigenous people live their lives.

I stayed awake deep into the night to watch multigenerational
men, clad in traditional Indonesian sarongs, lit up by
firelit lanterns, paddleboarding out to their crab traps, the
atmosphere wrapped in otherworldly silence. Always with the
first morning light the same men traded their catch for bamboo
poles, rice, maybe a nice piece of hand-dyed batik fabric from
Java. They made the entirety of their abodes from their local
and neighboring ecosystems and by practicing the ancient and
ever-present system of barter and trade.

The connection between people, place, and apparel has a history reaching all the way back past the Neanderthals. To learn more about the history of clothing, I reached out to Carroll Dunham — *National Geographic* explorer, author, anthropologist, and cofounder of Around the World in 80 Fabrics — for an absolutely fascinating exploration of the past, present, and future of fashion.

The oldest fabrics known to human beings, the "Big Five" as Carroll calls them, were created in part because of their unique ecosystems of plants and animals, and the fact that travel and trade was limited to small regions. Flax linen, cotton, animal products, and silk — each of the Big Five has an archeological record going back more than 30,000 years, and each of their material sources were found to be linked directly to the biodiversity of the area they were discovered. The Japanese fishermen wearing fish-skin leather, the artisan Muga silk from the Himalayas in Bhutan, even the hand-dyed batik fabric from Java, Indonesia, all have this same thing in common. It took thousands of years and the evolution of craftsmanship to bring us the gorgeous fabrics we have today.

But in the past century, our small, enclosed ecosystems and markets have given way to full-scale globalization at an accelerated rate that no one could have imagined. Globalization is loosely defined as the interdependence, on an international level, of the world's economy. That includes raw materials, manufacturing, agriculture, waste, and just about anything that can be made. This is why when you buy a shirt, it may say "Made in China," but it was likely grown in the Southeastern United States, woven in Bangladesh, sewn in China, and then stored in some warehouse internationally until it showed up in your mailbox.

What was once a world of separate and defined cultures and artisan fabrics is now a one-world ecosystem where once-sustainable farming practices have been traded for industrial agriculture. And where it was once considered a source of pride to be an artisan fabric-maker and seamstress, it is now one of the lowest-earning jobs in the world. I asked Carroll what she thinks of the globalization of the fashion industry as an anthropologist, and she has a lot to say about it.

Exclusive Interview with Carroll Dunham of *National Geographic*

CD: "So on one hand, it's a horrible thing. And on the other hand, what we just had with COVID, so many of the Indigenous communities we're talking with, they're very savvy. They're all plugged in; they've got their social media; they're able to see what's going on. So with that knowledge, there's less ability for exploitation and more ability to understand their value.

"The main issue is what globalization has done in communities. I'm down in Oaxaca, and it's only the older women that are wearing the old and the traditional beautiful clothes. They are also the only ones that have the whole tradition, where not only are they growing their Coyuchi cotton, they are processing it, and laboriously picking out all of those seeds; they are spinning it and wearing it. You know, that low-carbon footprint, that's a very rare thing to find in this world today.

"When you look at the journey of the clothing that most of us wear, that we're buying in our large American stores, that are coming to us via Amazon, you know, where the cotton comes from Uganda, and then it goes up to China. And then it goes down to Malaysia for finishing, you know, I mean, it's absolutely insane globalization, the carbon footprint in transportation alone.

"It's a hard fight. For example, my friend Raj has an amazing company called Seven Weeks, and they make the most extraordinary Eri silk. He says to me, 'Carroll, the economics don't work. Why do I say that? How can a human making something handcrafted, hand-spun, compete when you're trying to clothe the entire world? There's a reason we had an industrial revolution.'

"One of the most extraordinary revelations for me when studying the impact of industrialization was who took the biggest hit. It was women; women took the biggest hit. We know that for 20,000 years, weaving textiles has been a woman's work of art. Women used to be able to get a little of their own pocket change because they had their own little looms in their industries, etc. They were hand-making and living off commission. And with industrialization, that money was taken away from women and moved up into these larger mass scales.

"Globalization took away from localized small, tiny productions. And how do we change once we have gotten used to the price points of globalization? Who pays the price? The Earth, human rights, workers in developing worlds pay those prices. My husband was there in Bangladesh to document after the Rana Plaza* incident. The tragedy is real, and it's not finished yet. The fashion industry is one of the darkest corners of the economic world in terms of human rights. It's like one in six people on this planet are employed in the creation of textiles; this is a huge thing. Many people say that the textile fashion industry is our second largest polluter in the world. So there is a real need for us today to transform what we're wearing and our relationship to our clothes."

*The 2013 Rana Plaza factory collapse was a structural failure that occurred on 24 April 2013 in the Savar Upazila District of Dhaka, Bangladesh, where an eight-story commercial building called Rana Plaza collapsed. The search for the dead ended on 13 May 2013 with a death toll of 1,134.

"What I have learned during our explorations is when we look at what we've been wearing, I call them the Big Five, and I'm not referring to football teams, but I mean in textiles, you know, what is the oldest that we've been wearing? The oldest fiber we have found is actually flax, and I don't know if you've ever looked at a flax plant: it has a tiny little blue flower. I would not look at it and immediately say, 'You know what, I think I'm gonna wear that next season.' I mean, that is just not what's gonna happen.

"But we look at all the different fibers; it's absolutely astonishing when we go deep with microscopy, into the different fibers of the different Big Five. For example, when we look at animal or plant proteins, which are some of our earliest of the Big Five. In the coastal tundra they were harvesting seals. We think of seals being clubbed, but in fact, you know, for them in their environment, that's all there was. And so that is the pelt they would wear. We don't advocate that you go out and buy seal cloth; but to recognize and honor the different communities, what is appropriate in different ecosystems. To know what is sustainable, we have to look at ecosystems.

"Then there is wool, hemp, and of course, there is cotton. We've seen in Egypt cotton that is 5000 years old, and we have found it all over the world. Yet ironically, right now 90% of the cotton found on this planet is from the United States. But you can find the most beautiful forest cotton in Oaxaca, Mexico. It's not commercially planted so it doesn't take the kind of water required for industrial farms, it just takes whatever rain comes from the sky. And I was just in Bhutan two months ago, and we were finding other local indigenous varieties of cotton.

"We need to recognize the biodiversity possible within the Big Five as well. The last of which is silk. Silk is the biggest rabbit hole on the planet you'll go down. I was just in Assam less than a month ago, and in Assam, which is northeast India, they've been making the most expensive silk found on this planet called Muga silk. It has very iridescent, very golden qualities. They also have what's called the Brahmaputra ecosystem of the Eri silk moth which creates Ahimsa silk. It has a unique cocoon where you do not have to kill the pupae to make the silk like the Bombyx — which is more dry and the most common genus as we look at natural history.

"So we were there within the forest communities and their unique biology, their connection, their relationship to the silk. I mean, it's just mind-boggling to think of some of the heritage we've inherited from our ancestors. We came across an extraordinary moth brothel just filled with water and these huge, gigantic moths. They're so gorgeous. And the minute they emerge from the cocoon, they start to mate; and then the female lays the eggs on a little stick, and they make sure the human intervenes to put them up into a tree. They're very fussy eaters just the way we think of Bombyx eating mulberry leaves.

"And they have to watch to make sure the monkeys don't get them. Because the monkeys love to go up in the trees. Because they're so sticky, the cocoons, they stick them on their hair; and like thieves, they're covered with the cocoons, and they run down the trees to eat them.

"You do not have to kill the pupae to create Muga or Eri silk. But for these tribal communities, the pupa is an essential form of protein. So they actually will eat them. And some might say, 'Oh this is so horrible.' But we look to the future of what food is and people think that it may be insects. That is how we're going to survive with the massive populations we humans have here on this planet today. And what's so interesting with the tribes is, people come in and they want to commercialize their process, they want them to make a lot more money. But the tribespeople say, 'But I couldn't eat that many larvae.' Because there's a small period of time where they take them out of their cocoons. You can't dry them out; they have to eat them in a short period of three days.

"So why am I telling you all these long-drawn-out stories? Simply to share the extraordinary wonder of the ecosystems, and the natural history behind the clothes we wear. We're so cognizant, and we're becoming more aware of what we put into our bodies, with what we eat; and yet, we don't think very hard about what we're putting on our clothes. One of the huge takeaways is, how we can become more aware, not only of when we're buying, but what we're buying, and where it actually comes from."

I asked Carroll not as an anthropologist, but as a 20-year practicing Buddhist, if there are any mindfulness practices she would recommend to someone who enjoys buying cheap clothing so much it could qualify as an addiction. And she gave me this pearl.

CD: "I so appreciate that question. Because it has become an addiction, they have usurped the wiring of our neurological system. And now, with social media coming at you, buying clothes has become like a social video game. Buying in to win.

"In Buddhism, we often say, the way when you go into the British underground, 'Mind the gap.' Obviously, they're referring to the gap between the train and the platform; but in Buddhist practice, it refers to the idea of: Can we create space in the midst of the flow of our thoughts so that we can start to recognize our thoughts? See them. Separate from them. What are thoughts like? The Buddhists describe them as like logs in a river.

"Sometimes, some of us have very clogged rivers with lots of thoughts. In Tibetan Buddhism, they believe that to be human, we wouldn't be here if we didn't have a little greed, ignorance, and desire. And that's what gives us human form; that actually creates our humanity. But how skillfully we work with our own greed, our own ignorance, and our own desire impacts the quality of who we are as a human being. So how do we do that? How can we be skillful with that?

"First of all, just that simple notion of the pause. Can we slow down for one moment, and put a gap in space and go, 'Wait a second, do I really need that?'

"I know fast fashion is cheap. That's one of the reasons it's so addictive, just like fentanyl. Fentanyl kills, and fast fashion kills. Unfortunately, it's killing whole ecosystems; it's killing biodiversity. And we're sort of asleep to that. So there's good reasons to experiment and play with pausing before you buy, and feeling the abundance internally that we are nothing but loving kindness."

You can follow Carroll Dunham and her journey to match traditional and heirloom cultural practices from one tribe to the next through her nonprofit Around the World in 80 Fabrics. But you will hear more from her in the chapters ahead about the dangers of fast-fashion pollution and the future of fabrics.

Lifespan Meditation

By this time you have a better idea of the entire lifespan of your apparel, and your interconnectedness with yourself and the planet. Let's go deeper into that awareness.

Every person who touched your clothing on its way to you shared some of their energy in creating it, bringing a part of them to you in the experience. It is a startling thought to realize there are traces of energy that travel with your clothes before they even get to you, and reveals why it is important to understand where and how your apparel was made. Let's take it further with a visual exercise.

1. Choose two items from your closet. One that you treasure as a favorite style, and one that you wear literally all the time.
2. In a quiet place where you won't be interrupted, sit cross-legged with your treasured item in your hands. Look over it for details of the fabric, the seams that hold it together; read the tag to learn what it's made of and where it was made. Now close your eyes.

3. Remember when you first brought it home, how it felt to try it on. Now go back to when you first chose it — in a store or online — and trace the experience of the product when passing through different hands during delivery, holding overnight in a warehouse, being placed in a box from storage, and so on, or how it was placed in a bag when you drove it home to own.

4. Consider your article of clothing's lifetime on the shelf or on the rack. How long might that have been; who else wanted to buy it?

5. Now follow it as it arrived there, by car or by mail, and where it came from before that. Was it local to you? Was it sewn together overseas? Go to that country of origin in your mind and imagine that facility that packaged it, and who handled the packaging there.

6. Who put the tags on the garment, and the finishing touches? Who ran the pieces through a sewing machine to bind the shape? Who cut the shapes out of the fabric? Who made the pattern the fabric is modeled from?

7. Follow the fabric as it arrives at that facility in a roll or a hide. Now travel with the roll on a boat, a train, a car, to wherever the fabric was woven or tanned. Unroll it in a machine that is unthreading it mechanically with someone supervising. Watch as it becomes spools of thread. Watch the thread be taken off the machine and placed in a box to travel to where it came from.

8. The thread is now placed in a machine by a person, and it is unraveling into fibers; the fibers are having chemical treatments poured onto them, leaving just naked, raw material. Someone is managing this. Watch as it becomes a load of raw cotton, raw silk, just raw material. Or watch it being chemically untreated to become rawhide again.

9. Travel again with it to the place it was harvested or manufactured. Maybe you are at a farm in India, or

maybe you are at a petrol plant in Saudi Arabia. Follow the material until it is returned to the earth as a seed, a pocket of tar, or birthed into this world.

10. Reflect on all the people whose hands touched your favorite item, and what their lives were like. You are all connected by a physical object that had an incredible journey to get to you.

11. Repeat this process with the object you wear the most.

Journal

1. Write down what occurred to you during the reflection.

2. Contemplate your interconnectedness with the global world. Perhaps you never realized just how close you are to strangers of all lifestyles across the planet.

3. Repeat the lifespan meditation as often as you like, and with other items that you own. Jewelry, furniture, whatever you like. As you do this more often, you truly begin to understand what loop you are living in.

7

Leather and Wool

Two of the Big Five fabrics, leather and wool, have been used by humans for centuries. We've even uncovered leather moccasins that date back 5500 years.

Before the agricultural revolution, for most of human existence really, we have largely subsisted as hunters and gatherers without permanent residence. As a species, we evolved alongside the animals we hunted. We gained upright mobility and speed, and moved from being tree dwellers to apex predators on the vast plains of Africa. Part of the prize of the hunt was the luxurious skin and fur the animals would provide. We would use the skins to build structures to shelter us and clothes to keep us warm and protected from the bitter environment.

Modern leather feels luxurious and is a legacy piece that stays with you for decades. I remember as a teenager, when I had very little spending money, I prized my sister's leather jacket above all things in the closet of the household. So much so that I would "borrow" this jacket without her knowing and always get compliments. Even in college, a really nice leather jacket was something out of reach. I settled for the fake leather knockoff version and was fairly happy with it until it crumbled apart in my hands.

It wasn't until I was a fashion designer that I finally owned a sexy, black leather motorcycle jacket. And what made this one special is that it was something I designed. I sourced the lamb skin from a local farm in California, and it was dyed with vegetable dyes instead of heavy metals. The effort it took to create something made me very proud, and I will own it forever.

But as I asked more questions about sustainable fabrics, and the cleanest possible way of living, I came to this conundrum that I think a lot of people wonder about. What is worse for the planet: real leather, which has a massive carbon imprint, or plastic leather, which is a fossil fuel with its own set of environmental detriments?

On one hand, animal products have been a key part of humankind's early inventions. Like the old cliché "to use the whole buffalo," the byproduct of leather kept us warm for centuries and got us to where we are now. So how can something that has been used by people to clothe their bodies for so long become a problem? Patagonia would have you think that wool is totally sustainable, and yet PETA would tell you there's no way in hell it is. "Breeding and killing millions of animals is completely unnecessary at this point," claims Sienna Martz of PETA. "We have more amazing vegan options than we have ever had before."

I made a call to Sienna, head of communications at PETA, on a rainy day during the lockdown phase of the pandemic. I wanted to square away what I needed to know as a designer. Since I had used animal products in the past, I wanted to tread with knowledge into the new company I was founding. She answered swiftly and passionately.

Exclusive Interview with Sienna Martz of PETA

SM: "I've been the clothing campaign coordinator for PETA for a couple of years now. I coordinate media events, corporate campaigns, fashion campaigns, collaboration, runway shows, sustainability panels, and so much more, to really encourage business and consumers to choose vegan and sustainable fashion. It is at the heart of PETA that all living beings have the right to be free from exploitation. Our world is plagued with problems, and cruelty to animals is one of them.

"We've worked with so many amazing companies like Save the Duck, outerwear company Noize, Brave GentleMan. We've even worked with larger companies like Free People. We have a really long list of amazing brands that are either fully vegan or introducing vegan capsule collections."

CB: "How important is it to work with vegan products right now?"

SM: "I think the public is increasingly turning to vegan materials including faux furs and vegan leathers, and they are identifying sustainability as a key factor when choosing what brands they want to support and buy from. And we are seeing consumers, especially young consumers, becoming more aware that animals are individuals with feelings. They are learning that they are being abused for their skins, and the environmental impact of it all. They are choosing clothing and accessories that are ethically produced as well as functional, stylish, and far better for the environment. So any designer or brand that doesn't want to be left behind by this conscious consumer should really turn to these vegan materials."

CB: "What are some common myths about PETA?"

SM: "Especially because I work specifically with our clothing and fashion campaigns, one of the common myths is that PETA throws red paint and blood on people wearing fur. This is something they show in movies. We have often put red paint on ourselves to highlight cruelty during protests and demonstrations. The media often picks up on the more outrageous things that we do and it helps to open the door for a larger conversation."

CB: "Have you taken part in protests?"

SM: "I *have* taken part in protests! We have protests around the world! But I have protested Canada Goose in New York City. We did a protest outside a company whose headquarters are in Los Angeles. It is really exciting to come together as activists and see how the public is reacting. Learning about the information, especially about Canada Goose, we are encouraging consumers to boycott the company until the brand stops supporting the gruesome killing of geese and coyotes for their feathers and fur that they use for the jacket lining and stuffing. It is exciting to see consumers make the connection and become quite shocked.

"It depends on the campaign, what we do. Sometimes it is just positive interaction with the public. But specifically with Canada Goose we'll have folks out there with signage. Sometimes we show footage on computer screens of coyotes trapped and killed in the wild for a Canada Goose jacket. We had a colorful and lively Forever 21 demonstration about their use of wool, where we had someone dressed up in a wool costume educating people about how the wool industry is violently killing sheep.

"One of my favorite moments so far with PETA was with a partnership we did last year with WWD MAGIC, which is one of the largest women's trade shows in the United States. The trade show's 2019 theme was to educate the community about the growing number of conscious vegan products that are now available to them. PETA got involved with ethical brand Coalition LA and we hosted a really impactful, amazing vegan fashion panel with celebrity animal activist Daniella Monet."

CB: "You work in three-dimensional textiles as an artist as well. How did you get started with that?"

SM: "It's a beautiful thing to not only work for the largest vegan-forward organization in the world, but to have my focus with

PETA be with vegan fashion and textiles. I, as a vegan textile artist, have applied what I've learned to my art. My path kind of began with focusing on textiles and sculpture. The textile industry, especially in art, makes you believe you should buy alpaca and fur, and that these are the materials every artist should use. But the reality is so far from that, and I've really connected with dozens of vegan textile artists who believe that vegan textile is the way to go with our art process. I've blended my work with PETA and my work as a vegan textile artist to help get the message out there to other artists with the hope that they switch over."

CB: "So you only work with vegan textiles?"
SM: "As an ethical vegan it expands from what I eat, to what I wear, to how I entertain myself, what companies I support. It really reflects the same with my work as an artist. I make sure I am buying plant-based instead of synthetic. I will not work with any animal-derived material at all. And it feels really wonderful to know that my art is not hurting the environment and contributing to the deaths of millions of animals every year. I think a lot of artists don't make that connection with what they are buying."

CB: "How do people react to vegan art?"
SM: "I've had really wonderful reactions to my work — aesthetically, conceptually. I consider it a piece of vegan art. They get to question what that means. A lot of people are surprised and excited by the fact that these materials like wool, silk, and mohair shouldn't be used for art. It begins to make sense. I've also had a lot of textile artists reach out to me for guidelines and where they can buy plant-based textile materials, and I actually wrote an article on PETA's website highlighting all of the amazing brands around the world where people can find vegan textiles. And I gave a lot of shoutouts

to companies where you can find materials to make vegan art."

CB: "Where do we find you online?"
SM: "Anyone and everyone can reach out to me about what it is to be a vegan and a vegan artist. How to transition to being a vegan artist, and how to wear and be vegan. I am an open book if anyone wants to reach out."

CB: "What about wool and leather?"
SM: "In addition to causing the suffering and death of billions of animals every single year, the production of animal skins that includes leather, wool, fur, and other animal-derived materials is contributing to climate change, land devastation, soil degradation, air pollution, water contamination, and loss of biodiversity. There are so many beautiful and eco-friendly options out there that there is really no need to breed and kill millions of animals every year.

"Wool is far from sustainable. And I think a lot of people are starting to make this connection. There is a lot of new data coming out that shows wool emits extremely high levels of greenhouse gases, which makes wool a significantly more dangerous material than synthetic and plant-based products. PETA has released 12 exposés on over 100 shearing companies on four different continents, and all of them have revealed how sheep are systematically beaten, kicked, punched, and mutilated in the wool industry. And it proves this is an industry norm. Shearers typically are paid by the number of sheep they shear, which encourages this fast and violent work that leads to sheep having gaping wounds sewn shut by needle and thread. And a number of sheep who aren't considered profitable are sent to the slaughterhouse.

"But thankfully there are a lot of vegan wool options that are cozy and keep people warm without harming these beautiful animals and our planet."

CB: "Are wool and leather harmful to the environment?"
SM: "Research is coming forward that wool is actually more harmful for the environment than synthetic options. Synthetics still aren't the most eco-friendly alternatives, so there are some wool-free options coming out including vegan knits made from Tencel, which is a wood pulp. There are also ones being made from hemp, cotton, and soy-based fabrics that are also now known as vegetable cashmere. These are really beautiful alternatives that are becoming readily available, and I think consumers who are conscious of the environment and ethics are searching out these plant-based, vegan-friendly options.

"The leather industry has been a shocking reveal for not only myself and consumers, but also business. Because animal agriculture and methane and nitrous oxide products, which includes leather, are the leading contributors to greenhouse gas emissions. And a study found that more than 90% of leather's contribution to greenhouse gases is caused by land use associated with farming. The impact is coming from farming, and the actual tanning process is only around 10% of the environmental impact of leather.

"Cow leather is one of the most valuable coproducts. A lot of people think it's a byproduct, but it is in fact a coproduct of the meat industry. And hides make up the single largest component of this coproduct, which values at nearly 40% — and the Center for Environmental Strategy found that leather accounts for 7–8% — of the total value of a cow, which is very significant. And as a result of the dropping value of leather in recent years, slaughterhouses and the leather industry in general are reporting a heavy economic loss. It really shows that these two industries are coexisting with each other economically."

CB: "Where does leather come from?"
SM: "Most leather originates from India, Bangladesh, and China, where millions of cows and other animals are killed for

their skins and endure all the horrors of factory farming, without any painkillers. Actually, in China, roughly 2 million dogs and cats every single year are killed for their skins, for leather, and for fur. And these products are being intentionally mislabeled and being sold to consumers around the world, including the US. So when you buy leather it can be mislabeled intentionally, and you really don't know who your leather is made out of.

"Ninety percent of the Amazon rainforest has been cleared to make way for pastures or for growing feed crops; livestock pollution is the greatest threat to our waterways, with factory farms accounting for 70% of the water pollution in the US."

CB: "What else is dangerous in leather production?"
SM: "Treating leather is an even more serious threat to the natural environment and people that rely on local water sources for their daily life. It is so toxic that the majority of tanning facilities have been moved out of Europe and the US to India and other countries in Southeast Asia. The typical chemicals used to treat leather include formaldehyde; coal tar derivatives; and cyanide-based oils, dyes, and finishes. Most tanneries use chromium, which is considered highly dangerous by the EPA. Chromium wastewater is incredibly carcinogenic, and can cause open skin sores and lung cancer. The case Erin Brockovich fought and won in Hinkley, which inspired the movie, is a famous US-based case of chromium poisoning within a community; though it was being used for another purpose than tanning, it is a good example of how extreme its effects are."

CB: "What about vegan leather?"
SM: "Comparing that with vegan leather, data from the Higg Materials Sustainability Index found that in three environmental impact categories — water scarcity, climate change, and eutrophication — cow leather is worse than vegan leather. Specifically, it reported an environmental impact score of

159 for cow leather, compared to an impact score of 59 for polyurethane (PU) leather; in other words, cow leather has almost three times the negative environmental impact of PU. Because of the greenhouse gas emissions created in its production, animal leather has a more significant impact on climate change than its synthetic counterparts.

"In addition, leather has the greatest impact on eutrophication, a serious ecological problem in which runoff waste creates an overgrowth of plant life in water systems, which suffocates animals by depleting oxygen levels in the water and is the leading cause of hypoxic zones, aka dead zones."

CB: "What about fur and down?"

SM: "Many of the global emissions associated with animal agriculture are shared with the fur and down industries. Fur has a high price. Producing 1 kg of fur has a CO_2 equivalent factor of about 130–140 kg, compared to faux fur at about 6–7 kg. Another hidden pollutant is water contamination by fecal matter. In 2013, a Washington State mink farm was charged with polluting a local creek with a fecal content level as much as 240 times higher than the legal limit. Even more disturbing, the chemicals used to tan the hides leach onto the wearer's skin, transferring cancer-causing chromates, ammonia, formaldehyde, hydrogen peroxide, and bleaching agents. Once contact with the skin has been made, it can take over 20 years to flush it out naturally.

"The amount of biowaste left behind is enough to turn a stomach. Farmed birds produce large amounts of manure that is collected in enormous pits called lagoons, which often leak and are linked to *E. coli*, bacteria, and other contaminants. Farms that focus on the fatty product foie gras can have birds that produce over 5 lb of fecal matter a day. That's a lot of toxic shit."

Alternatives to Expectations

As we will learn later on, the debate on leather versus "pleather" (plastic leather) is still ongoing. But Sienna made startling points about the environmental impact of animal products that we cannot ignore. And leather, being hailed as a luxury item, is almost always more expensive than your average clothing purchase even though we have more hides available to purchase than people.

And when it comes to designer brands, they almost exclusively use leather. For something you want really badly, like a handbag or a new leather jacket, you might have to save your paycheck for weeks to get it. The anticipation can be sweet, and you imagine that when you own it, the feeling will be even better.

The reality is different. Psychologist Daniel Gilbert and author of *Stumbling on Happiness* says, "Part of us believes that the new car is better because it lasts longer. But in fact, that's the worst thing about the new car. It will stay around to disappoint you." The things you own stick around, and you get used to them. After a while, they no longer spark joy. That is the case for my sister's leather jacket from the early 2000s; it is presently deep in a closet gathering dust.

We have a common misconception regarding how much joy we will experience once we own something.

The amount of anticipation leading up to buying something, which can be stressful in itself, can turn out to be more satisfying than actually owning that thing. That is because of a little thing called hedonic adaptation.

We as humans tend to move on from both positive and negative experiences very quickly. Getting into the college we want, losing a pet, getting the job we want, being broken up with — whatever our level of happiness was before that experience is where we tend to land after the experience of acquisition or loss is over. And the acquisition of stuff is on the list of experiences that undergo hedonic adaptation.

So how can we overcome this cognitive bias and thwart hedonic adaptation?

It is with our experiences that we stay longer in the sweet state of anticipation, rather than material things. Stop investing in nonessential items to secure your happiness. Start investing in experiences. Better yet, find free experiences happening in your area, and then when you need to invest in essential things, you will have the savings to do so.

It's okay to like nice things. In reality, no matter if it is a leather product or an alternative like pineapple leather, these kinds of goods are comparatively expensive. It's best to buy them only when you need them, and not to chase a short-lived spike of dopamine. The longer-lasting relationship with happiness is linked to your experiences.

Choose Your Own Experience

This week you are going to set aside time that you would usually use for online shopping and replace it with an experience.

Maybe in the evenings after dinner, you like to browse your favorite shops for wardrobe ideas. Catch yourself in the act. And instead, call a friend over for a movie and popcorn night. Or if you like to go to the mall or a shopping center on your breaks at work, instead go to a park and journal, or go on a hike. Simply look for times in your life when you would usually go shopping, and turn that into time devoted to experience.

You need to break the habit of screen and storefront time. So go ahead and make a list of five experiences you can do to break up the old time used. Perhaps you start looking for your next vacation. Or tour dates for your favorite band. Keep the list rolling, and add to it when you have finished all the actions.

In the online forum, in [Choose Your Own Experience] share with others what you successfully swapped out.

Journal

1. Reflect on "Choose Your Own Experience." What were the challenges that came up when you started? How often did you find yourself reverting to your old habits? How did you feel after converting shopping into experiences? How many experiences were you able to complete?
2. Contemplate the types of experiences you had this week. Is there an experience that would make you feel even better? Sit and feel into it; let the question speak to you. This will help you add to your list for later experiences.
3. Meditation: Find a quiet place on your own, sit down cross-legged if it is comfortable, and close your eyes for ten minutes. Focus on your breath, letting it guide you to the place of quiet and openness. Focus on the openness inside you, the place that is longing for new experiences. Breathe into it, and feel its largeness. Find where that space is all over your body; breathe into it.

8

Greenwashing

And though you seek in garments the freedom of privacy, you may find in them a harness and a chain.

— Kahlil Gibran, *The Prophet*

Now that we know more about the global impact of the fashion industry — through both emissions and dyes, and just how tied together it all is with the supply chain — let's pull back the curtain on why some of our basic instincts tell us to buy cheap clothes even when we know they aren't good to begin with, and how big business is taking advantage of it all to boot. Then we will work to undo this mess.

Have you noticed how suddenly every company is proclaiming themselves to be "for the environment" and "a part of the solution"? I'm glad you are paying attention. Chances are that only a few among them are doing anything of any value to improve their actual supply chain and are simply greenwashing their image to make themselves look better.

Greenwashing, according to Greenwash.com, is a term used to explain "the practice of falsifying or overstating the green credentials of a product, service, or brand," or even a company itself.

Greenwashing is increasingly widespread and can be found across numerous sectors from food and fashion to energy, electronics, and finance. It can be done in a subtle way, for example through the use of logos and colors, or by omitting certain information to give the impression that a product is more environmentally friendly than it really is. Or it can take the form of broad, vague claims placed on products, for example "carbon-neutral," "sustainable," or "responsible."

My first clash with the thin veil of greenwashing happened right from the start of launching my first eco-friendly business. After hours of searching online for local fabric stores in the greater Los Angeles area that might have something "sustainable," I made the traffic-congested drive to the outskirts of the city to inspect a warehouse.

I picked out a few promising wovens for T-shirts, and a nice denim for a men's button-up, and as I searched it was surprising to find fabrics qualifying as eco-friendly that contained less than a third of organic materials. But there they were! Upon asking about it, the fabric makers said that it was perfectly fine to advertise it that way because the company who make the fiber Tencel only require a third of their product to be in a fabric before it can use their official logo and seal of approval.

You see, Lenzing make this wonderful fabric out of eucalyptus pulp that goes by the name of Tencel, and it is all the rage in sustainable fashion. It was alarming to find you could weave Tencel with plastic fibers and still call it Tencel with Lenzing's stamp of approval. It's like calling a shark a tuna fish, just because it ate tuna fish for lunch. It's still a shark.

Greenwashing is disturbing because it misuses the good faith of consumers who want to do the right thing. It is just enough to make a company look good without doing anything meaningful. It can actually do a considerable amount of harm because it funnels your well-intended money into the exact same system you are trying to change.

Carroll Dunham, the medical anthropologist, Buddhist chaplain, and social entrepreneur we met in the previous chapter, saw this as well. "There's an enormous amount of greenwashing going on right now. So you can say, oh, but this is cactus leather. Well, I would ask you to look at that cactus leather, and ask how much is cactus? See, they know that people are going to be lazy, they're just going to put a little drop of cactus into a petroleum product. That is a serious, serious problem. It's like faux leather, because I think one of the worst greenwashers that we have is this notion of vegan leather. That is a joke. It's polyester. I mean, it's ridiculous. It's a petroleum-based product, no two ways about it. And so we have to just read clothing labels the same way we read food labels. I think it's really essential as we move forward."

You can do your due diligence and check your favorite brands on www.greenwash.com, backed by Extinction Rebellion founder and climate campaigner Bel Jacobs, whom I have interviewed about naysayers. The website includes numerous examples of fashion greenwashing by brands such as H&M, Boohoo, Zalando, M&S, Nike, Primark, Puma, and Adidas. They take a hard line on anything remotely promoting plastic, even recycled plastics, but it helps you get a clearer picture of what is going on.

Greenwashing is not going to go away anytime soon. Why? We need to remember that behind these huge companies are individual people. It is people who are claiming false identities. Why would someone claim to be something when they are not? It is a part of the same reason we buy fast fashion to begin with, and we are going to take a deep dive into the human mind to find out more.

The Second Noble Truth of ReFashion: The Cause of Suffering

Remember, the First Noble Truth of ReFashion is that the planet is suffering. The Second Noble Truth of ReFashion is that the cause of suffering is desire, or craving pleasure, material goods, and immortality. All of which are wants that can never be satisfied.

How does desire manifest itself in the fashion industry? Each of us has within us an emptiness or a feeling of lack. Within that emptiness is where desire operates like a machine, pulling in things for us to attach to. It is one of the ways we create an identity; we attach ourselves to the objects that bring us what we desire. Sometimes the objects themselves are what we desire. The way we look, the way we dress, the amount of things we own — the machine of desire pulls in more and more to fill this hole that constantly tells us we are not enough.

In the global West, culturally we have agreed that if we dress a certain way, drive a certain car, and make a certain amount of money, we will suddenly feel whole and accepted. Advertisers know this and present to you a hundred different outfits you could buy to feed this lie — that owning just the right things will make you enough. Worse, they have tapped into your desire to do better and so they present you with "eco-friendly clothes for the environment" that aren't safe for the planet at all.

There is no clothing on this planet you could ever buy that will fill that emptiness. Desire sits right at the top of that void as a necessary evil to keep us motivated. But the question is, how do we navigate our desire skillfully? How do we reform our relationship with desire so that it is no longer harming the planet or ourselves?

That emptiness is actually a key part of you that is ripe for spiritual growth. It is the quiet, it is the witness, and it is itching to be touched. When Carroll Dunham said to "mind the gap," I loved it. It is in that empty space that true richness lies. If you can give yourself a breath and lean into the darkness that is there, you will find it is the door to enter our knowing, inner silence, and inner peace. The place that can scare us is the fear of not having enough, the fear of not being accepted because I'm not wearing the latest fashions. How can we accept ourselves as having enough, as being enough?

I look at some of my clothes and see stains and frayed edges, and I wear wrinkled linen out in the world like it's not a thing. I'm constantly discovering new ways to embrace and cherish the experience of wearing my clothes until they can no longer be worn. That is actually being radical in today's world. How strange is it that accepting oneself can be radical? How can we push it further by being compassionate to ourselves?

Ask yourself, "Who am I dressing for in the first place?" Am I dressing to feel differently about myself, to fill a hole or a desire that is not really about clothes?

To you the earth yields fruit, and you shall not want if you but know how to fill your hands. It is in exchanging the gifts of the earth that you shall find abundance and be satisfied. Yet unless the exchange is in love and kindly justice, it will but lead some to greed and others to hunger.
— Kahlil Gibran, *The Prophet*

Meet Your Ego: Whom Are You Dressing For?

You are going to check in with yourself in a moment. In this questionnaire, you are to answer according to how you behave right now. This is for your self-reflection; there is no wrong answer.

Respond to the following statements:

3 – This is me **almost all** of the time
2 – This is me **some** of the time
1 – This is me **a little** of the time

__ When I go shopping, I need a friend there to approve of my choices.

__ I follow fashion influencers online to help me know what to buy.

__ I have changed my look to please someone I dated.

__ I care a lot about what people think of my appearance.

__ Every Halloween costume I buy could be seen as sexy.

__ I wear outfits in the hopes of receiving compliments.

__ On my social media, I wear a different outfit in each picture.

__ It is important to me to be known as stylish.

__ My friends and I all have a similar style.

__ I often buy straight-off-the-runway looks.

__ I have a celebrity style idol whom I model my closet after.

__ My look could be considered on-trend.

__ I change my look to fit in with my different friend groups.

__ I buy from fast-fashion websites to get expensive-looking clothes very cheap.

__ I invest in a new wardrobe quarterly to match the latest trends.

__ I go out of my way to look cute when I am meeting new people.

__ I have dozens of options for the same fashion object: sunglasses, sneakers, and so on.

__ Only fresh, new clothes appeal to me.

__ My look would not be considered timeless.

__ I have an outfit for all occasions.

__ A good amount of my wardrobe could be considered revealing.

__ Brand labels are important to me.

__ I dress up often.

__ It takes me over 30 minutes to get ready.

__ I don't repeat the same outfit often.

There is no right or wrong here. The point is to see where you are and what influences your shopping habits.

Evaluating your score

0–25 points: Wow! You have a very clean self-esteem that isn't rooted in society at all. How the fashion industry operates is of little interest to you. You are likely an influence to others just because you are so original.

26–35 points: You are fairly free from the pressures of society when it comes to your wardrobe. This allows you total creativity when you put together outfits without the ego influencing the outcome. You mostly dress for yourself, and sometimes for special occasions. It must be nice to not care about what people think. You could benefit from simply changing what it is you buy in the future.

36–40 points: You have a taste for what is trending and you want people to notice. Being seen helps your self-esteem, and you and your friends likely have a similar style. Sharing similar taste with your friends can come in handy when you want to trade something out without buying anything new. Be mindful that you don't always have to fit in.

41–51 points: You have society in your blood. Being a walking fashion statement fuels your identity. The fashion influence you have on others is remarkable; people look to you for ideas. Going sustainable could help you stand out even more. Just be careful that your intention isn't centered on the need for attention. All the validation you need comes from heart wisdom — the quiet internal knowledge that you are walking in line with the planet and its people. ReFashioning is entirely for you and your personal integrity.

Share

Share your results in the ReFashion Workshop Online Classroom [Meet Your Ego] discussion board in the Greenwashing chapter.

Give us a summary of what habits led you to that bracket, and what it makes you think about. Reflect on how you dress for other people, and how you might change that to better reflect who you want to be.

Journal

1. Reflect on the category you fell into during the "Meet Your Ego" exercise. What category was it? Do you feel like it describes who you are right now? Did you notice things about yourself that you might not have noticed otherwise? Does it call to mind the behavior of friends and acquaintances? Are you compelled to work on your habit of dressing for others?

2. Contemplate on what it would feel like if you dressed only for yourself. What would that look like? How would it differ from how you style yourself right now?

3. Meditation: For the next ten minutes, sit in a quiet place with your eyes closed, and focus on your breath to lead you to a state of calm and awareness. Listen to the beat of your heart; feel the rhythm of your body, the pulsation of nerves, the movement of blood circulating. Let yourself feel your personal rhythm and vibration of your still and alive body. You are coming back in touch with your awareness of your unique place in the universe as a living being.

9

Holding Court

Treating the planet as if we plan to stay, but open to cosmic connections.

— Courtney Barriger

I get a tingling sensation whenever I talk about the brand I've built, Holding Court, purely because it is exactly where I want to be. My brand is more than a place to shop for clothes. In my short time kicking on planet Earth, I've gone the distance in self-discovery and found that the values I most return to are wisdom, adventure, beauty, creativity, and seeking the profound unknown. The more time I spend in my values, the more I desire to express what I've experienced with storytelling and art. I can't help but create. And over the years, I've taken every creative expression I have — aesthetics, drawing, writing, building, designing and producing, even photography and acting — and channeled it into one conceptual place, Holding Court. It holds all the hope that I wish to inspire other people with, and the love I give of myself.

If you were to flip through a photo album of all the shenanigans I've gotten into in business in the arts, you might say I am all over the place. I spent my college years writing books and making fine art for galleries. And then many focused years only modeling and commercial acting. And then there is a whole span where I produced and directed short films. And through each phase of creative expression, I end up crossing over into other avenues here and there. But I decided to channel all of it, plus what I have studied in my spiritual and environmental practices, into one place. Holding Court.

Holding Court sends you vibrations of retro cool, relaxed and natural. It's aspirational and high frequency. It inspires me to continue to push forward with integrity and purpose. The need for change in the fashion industry and the opportunity to create a shift in our cultural zeitgeist is tangible. It's something I feel inside me, and I am playing my role in creating a brand that is beautiful and accessible. And just like me, my brand loves sharing information on the eco fashion movement and living life with the fullest expression.

The future of the company will change as I change, sometimes focusing more on film and storytelling, sometimes focusing more on design. But it will always be a place that will hold court on improving our relationship with Mother Earth by inviting a planet-healing mindset.

In shaping and creating structure, and imagining how I would be able to bring all my favorite things into one place, I came up with "The Threefold Path: Give/Take/Story." It didn't happen by accident, or overnight. I went deep inside myself and asked how I could make sense of the infinity of sustainability rhetoric, and make it actionable. So I broke it up into three stages that all feed into each other.

Give

The act of giving yourself happens automatically just by existing, as does taking. What you give comes in the form of action. Everything that you do with your speech, your hands, your feet, your sex, and your mind creates expectations and hopes for the future. This is how you give of yourself. In Samkhya philosophy it is called the Karmendriyas. Your giving is how you touch the world, and it is the imprint you leave behind as you go. It is the exhalation from your lungs that nourishes plant life with your carbon dioxide. It is the beautiful scarf you gifted your friend for her birthday that left her with a feeling of love.

To put it even more plainly, how you give of yourself is how you express your love. Love is a verb, it is an action, and when you give of yourself in the wrapping of love, you raise the vibration of the world around you. Love as a vibration has been monitored scientifically. I asked my friend Mickaela Grace, founder of the emotional intelligence and consciousness school Graceline Institute, what she has discovered in her research of higher vibrations. She said: "In my studies to know our emotions on an energetic level, it has been studied with instruments, and it shows fear to be the lowest emitter of energy, and love to be the highest incarnation of it."

When you give of yourself with love, you receive love in return. Accessing love in the realm of fashion would be giving only Earth-friendly clothing as gifts to your loved ones. It would be researching the most loving way to release your unwearable clothes, which could look like using old cotton shirts in planter beds, tailoring an old dress to become something new, or finding a clothing recycling box instead of throwing it in the trash. Think of everything you own as an extension of yourself and how you love yourself. Because it is.

Take

The act of taking from the world is also as natural as inhaling oxygen. In Samkhya philosophy it is called the Inanendriyas, or the use of the five senses (touch, sight, taste, sound, and smell). It is the act of receiving and utilizing the physical world as it comes to us. We didn't evolve to have a coat of fur to protect us, and so we take from the environment what we need to clothe ourselves and protect our bodies from the sun, wind, and cold.

We should take what we need to live and be happy with as much awareness as we give. And to do that in integrity with our highest potential of living with love, we need to choose the clothes that cause the least harm to people and the planet. Because what we take from the world in turn becomes what we give.

Story

Give and take are cyclical and completely intertwined. And when you add the third level, the story you tell yourself, you will see how all three of them must be aligned if you are to refashion your life.

The stories we create for ourselves are incredibly powerful, like a primitive drumbeat, irresistibly moving us along. Stories are both instinctual and intellectual in that they can spring forward unbidden, change in a moment, and are also finely crafted when we are alone with ourselves. Just like our ego, our personal stories are a form of protection and safety. They help create a familiar form for us to understand ourselves and be able to share ourselves with others.

Stories are alive. Just like a living organism, they reproduce! Think of one childhood game of telephone, and tell me this isn't true. One good story can be told a thousand different ways. Just look at the book *The Hero with a Thousand Faces* by the late Joseph Campbell, where he demonstrates that one story format shows up again and again in oral history, literature, and now film. And it is a form we all relate to.

More often than not, we tend to see ourselves as the hero of our own story. We are the person the world is effecting change on; and ultimately it is up to us to save the day for our romantic partners, our children, ourselves, or our community. The hero often has a powerful enemy, a moral high ground, or a prerogative that gives them purpose.

When you fully step into the power of mindful giving and taking, you will instantly begin to change your story. It comes with knowledge. In this case, knowledge of the impact your choices have on people and the environment shapes the narrative landscape. You become an eco-warrior, a steward of the planet; your identity now has a new purpose, and the rest of your life will fall in line with it. This is why it is so important to take this on fully and incorporate it into your story. Because then it becomes you at the most impactful level possible, and you will enact change without even thinking about it. It becomes your core purpose.

I have applied the Threefold Path to my lifestyle and the business I created, making three divisions to address each aspect with care and dedication.

To Give Sustainably, I have created Environmental Style Now — [E.S.Now] — a division of Holding Court devoted to education in sustainable fashion. It began as a blog that has now evolved into this book. But every month I interview a new scientist, policymaker, activist, or awesome person interested in the cause of a better way to make clothes, and I share it on my podcast of the same name: *E.S.Now.* And whenever I get the chance, I'll offer to give a talk or a lecture on eco fashion to any person or classroom willing to listen.

To Take Sustainably, I have meticulously chosen fabrics and manufacturers that meet my criteria for clean fashion to create the retro mystic threads that make my brand Holding Court special. We take from the planet only organic, nontoxic fabrics that you can throw into your compost when you are done with them.

Finally, to Tell Stories about Sustainability, I've developed projects over the past decade to spark conversations about sustainability in fashion. From fashion films to children's books, I believe if we change our popular culture we have a much greater chance of making an impact in the household.

If I can find ways to apply this to my life in a large way, you can find simple ways to change what you give and take with your wardrobe. One way you can understand specifically what you take is to learn more about what you want and need in general. You are going to take a personality survey to help you dig deeper into your inner world.

Dress for Your Personality

Do you ever look into your closet and think, "These looks don't fit my personality anymore"? Just like our bodies reinvent themselves every seven to ten years, so do our personalities. For many of us, there are core attributes that stay forever, but every four years or so on average, people undergo a cycle of personality shift. And this shift eventually appears in the way you style yourself.

Maybe you used to dress in a sexier way, but now you feel a strong urge to appear more professional. Or maybe you used to play it safe in your color palette but are currently feeling more playful and expressive in color.

When you look into your closet, do you see the old version of yourself? When you go shopping, do you buy whatever strikes your eye, or do you have a plan? It makes a big difference in your carbon footprint to have an outline of your style ahead of time so you buy outfits you will actually wear. Selective buying not only saves you money; it also lowers your carbon footprint by lowering your consumption.

Who are you right now? And how can you dial in those attributes to represent your personal style?

Personality Survey

The link below will take you to a personality survey by the VIA Institute on Character. In 15 minutes or less, this survey will reveal your greatest strengths. Knowing these will help you know yourself a little more, and help you direct your style habits.

The VIA survey is a scientifically validated survey that is regarded as a central tool of positive psychology. It's been used in hundreds of research studies and taken by over 8 million people in over 190 countries — free, because they believe everyone should be able to harness the power of their most positive traits.

While often simplified as grit or self-control, character is more than simply individual achievement or a person's behavior. It is a broad and complex family of thoughts, feelings, and behaviors that are recognized and encouraged across cultures for the values they cultivate in people and society. Character is the aggregate of who we are; it's what's inside every one of us.

Character strengths aren't about ignoring the negative. Instead, they help us overcome life's inevitable adversities. For example, you can't be brave without first feeling fear; you can't show perseverance without first wanting to quit; you can't show self-control without first being tempted to do something you know you shouldn't.

The results are private and confidential. Go on, take the test.

In the ReFashion Online Workshop, follow the link to [Character Strengths Survey].

Journal

1. Reflect on the top five results from your personality test. Write them down in your journal. If you feel the top ten are a more rounded version of you, write down all ten. Let yourself embrace the positive feelings of all the personality traits.

2. Contemplate the situations where you embodied these personality traits. Where have there been patterns in your life? Where do you seek them out? Which people appear when you feel it the most? Take a moment or two

to write down your answers for each personality trait. If you feel strongly about traits that make it past the top five, put them down too.

3. Evaluate the following basic areas of life and make a note of where your personality traits show up:

- Food / diet
- Physical activity / exercise
- Home environment
- Work environment
- Career
- Sleep
- Partnership relationships
- Family relationships
- Friendships
- Work relationships
- Interests / books / TV / websites / entertainment

4. Open up your closet and take an honest look at what is inside. Does your apparel make you feel connected to who you are as a personality? What matches up? What doesn't match up? Set aside the garments that no longer serve you. Take your time; you don't have to do it all in one day. This is a gradual process. Keep them to the side for a later date — we have a place for them.

5. Meditation: For ten minutes, sit in a quiet place where no one will disturb you. Close your eyes and breathe deeply into your chest, letting each breath calm and focus your mind into exquisite silence. Scan your body with your breath. You have so much personality that wants to express itself. Where is it resting in your body? Seek it out with your breath, and when you find something that has a story, focus there. Feel it in its entirety. Your

personality lives in you, and so it occupies space. With your breath, let it strengthen and fill you. Give it more space to express itself.

Accountability

Share with your accountability partner the results of your VIA Institute on Character personality survey. Be excited! You just uncovered new mysteries about yourself! Send them a link to the site if they are curious to take the test themselves.

In the ReFashion Workshop online, go to the [Dress for Your Personality] page, and share with us about one item in your closet that no longer serves your personality. Tell us what is your strongest character trait, and how you imagine you might wear it on your sleeve. Literally.

10

Innovation

A Journey into the Future of Fabrics

The future of fashion innovation happens at the cross section between fashion and technology. What is created can reshape what we imagine is possible to put on our bodies and may even impact how we see our own identities, thanks to the development of augmented reality.

When I look to the future I get excited to see brand-new exotic fabrics made of waste products like coconut husks and fish skin becoming the new norm. I see a resurgence of old technology like cloth made of bark, or nettle-woven linen with a new spin on it. I see fantastic plastic polyester fading out because it is not a renewable resource; it isn't sustainable. In my conversation with Carroll Dunham, with her focus on the wisdom of Indigenous cultures and cutting-edge innovations in recycling and biofabrication, I asked her which innovative fabrics she is most excited about. And it really blew my mind.

"I'll give you a couple of them," she said over Zoom one chilly winter morning. "So we have a project where we look at animal proteins, plant proteins, biofabricated fibers, recycled and upcycled materials. We're really focused on the biological impact these fabrics make.

"Let me tell you a fun and wild sexy one that everyone is amazed by: spider silk. It's an amazing, beautiful piece. I don't know if any of you have ever seen it. It's a dress that became famous and traveled through the Victoria and Albert Museum and other museums and is made from Madagascar spider silk. It's just extraordinary, and it opens a world of possibility.

"Another that is really interesting is using our human hair. Human hair is a renewable resource: think about how much we cut off our own heads every month, right? There are people who are spinning and making thread from human hair. One company is called Human Material Loop. Their first project product they're going to make is sneakers, but they have made sweaters as well, and who knows what is possible. Different ethnicities produce different hair, so there are actually many qualities we can choose from. It's all fiber. They're actually using hair mats right now to help soak up oil spills. So they're using them in city drains to absorb oil runoff from vehicles. And then they cut it nine to one, and they compost them at the end to soak up more petroleum waste. Just think of how hair can soak up oil. So I'm just giving you some that are sort of fun and strange and unusual.

"At our project Around the World in 80 Fabrics we just love lotus. If you look in Vietnam, Cambodia, and Myanmar, they actually make fiber from the stock of the lotus and they make it into fabric.

"And then there is the whole microbial world. An entire revolution is happening there in the field of biofabrication. It's an extraordinarily exciting time period, as they are experimenting and brewing up new clothes, so to speak, creating new polymers. You know, we think of how we're just coming out of COVID — our human relationship to microbes may either kill us or they may save us. In reality, we think microbes could be a companion species to humans. I mean, 98% of our bodies are microbes. So now we're looking at how we could create the new telomeres for the clothing of the future from microbes.

"There's also algae; they're making some really interesting things there. There are groups out of Israel doing interesting things out of orange waste. In India they're making things out of agricultural waste; I find that one super-interesting — fabric is made out of coconut waste. So these are feeding the microbes; for example, food waste or agricultural waste. They can actually take the DNA now out of indigo, for example, and make microbial dyes rather than synthetic dyes. So it's a very interesting new world. These are some of the things that get us very excited."

The idea of growing a dress in a Petri dish seems like something from science fiction, but it is truly happening right now, and could solve some of our most challenging problems with fashion pollution. Another way we look to the future of fashion is with Augmented Reality (AR). AR is the true merging of technology and fashion within the virtual world.

Consider how many people play video games and immerse themselves in social media as a pastime. Now imagine if that same group of people derived just as much satisfaction buying a virtual outfit as they do purchasing one in the physical world. I personally know people with a larger digital closet for their AR and VR avatars than they have in real life.

While it is not safe to lose yourself completely to the digital world, it is a safe way to change the way you look without impacting the planet or its people in a negative way.

Here are a few other innovative products hitting the market to look forward to:

- **BioGlitz:** This amazing company makes the world's only biodegradable glitter. Made from eucalyptus, this natural product will ideally replace microplastics.

- **ECONYL:** They recycle nylon from industrial waste like broken fishing nets and landfill stockings.
- **Flocus:** This company produces yarns and fillings made from the kapok tree, using trees that can be grown without using pesticides and in arid soil unsuitable for agriculture. This is a safe alternative to cotton.
- **Frumat:** Using apple pectin, this brand is creating a sustainable leather that is perfect for handbags and belts. Apple skin is a leather alternative made from the skin and core waste recovered from the food industry. Frumat was the winner of this year's Technology and Innovation Award at the Green Carpet Fashion Awards in Milan. The material contains a minimum of 50% apple fiber and is created in Bolzano, Italy.
- **Mango Materials:** The company produces biodegradable bio-polyester that can be used as a sustainable alternative to the polyester presently utilized in the fashion industry. Microfibers produced from the biopolyester can biodegrade in many environments, including landfills, wastewater treatment plants, and the oceans, helping to prevent microfiber pollution and contributing to a closed-loop bio-economy for the fashion industry.
- **Microsilk:** After studying the composition of spider webs, Microsilk has created a lab-grown fiber that mimics the strength and silkiness of a spider's web. No spiders were harmed during this process.
- **PlanetCare:** This company has produced a new nanoparticle filter that can be used in washing machines and in drains to capture loose microfibers that would otherwise make it into our oceans.
- **Provenance Bio:** Bioengineers have created leather without harming a hair on an animal. They use a scientific process that grows leather in a lab.

When I consider how creative the human mind is, and how much love is put into designing clothing, I can't help but be hopeful for the future. Sustainable fashion is still in its cradle; but as it learns to walk, I hope I get to be there when it is running. That is a thought that makes me truly happy. You know what can make *you* happy? As I refashioned my life from being a fashion-hoarding model in the clutches of the industry, I learned a few tricks to bump up my happiness even when I felt crushed by the impossible task of influencing change. I'll fill you in on what I learned.

Happiness

As I talked about in the last chapter with the Second Noble Truth of ReFashion, we often think that if we only had more possessions, we would feel more confident and complete. It's an ongoing struggle, the desire for material things and the mountains we move to get them. The elephant in the room, capitalism, is one of the strongest influences on how we find meaning in our lives. It prepares us from birth to enter a world where we are judged by what we own, so we spend the majority of our time chasing the acquisition of stuff. Pop culture hammers this in. Luxury goods become a symbol of status. They become a way we gauge our status in the world and directly affect our level of happiness.

Maybe you drive a really nice car, or have a killer salary that makes you feel like you have reached a strong level of success. Sonja Lyubomirsky, in her wonderful book *The How of Happiness*, says that no matter what your salary is, you will think you need more than double that to have a happy life. If you make $30,000 a year, you will think you need $65,000. If you make $100,000 you will want to make $250,000. No matter what you have, you will always think that having more will make you happier.

As humans, we tend to determine how well we are doing by the people around us. Maybe your neighbor got an amazing new pair of designer sunglasses, and suddenly your $15 frames don't make you so happy anymore. With the interconnectedness of social media and TV programming, we have blurred the lines even more. You may not be envious of your neighbor anymore; instead you might actually compare yourself to Lady Gaga — someone who may be far beyond your income bracket. This can lead to spending outside of your means, a very Western problem, and conditioning your mind to entitlement. Neither of these things is the path to happiness and full awareness.

This is a well-laid trap. You have the intuition that if you have the wardrobe you want, that expensive, luxurious look will make you happier. It is just wrong.

In *The How of Happiness*, Sonja Lyubomirsky explores how to get the kind of life that will bring you the most happiness. When it comes to happiness, there is a simple breakdown of components that lead to total fulfillment:

- 50% is your genetic makeup
- 40% is your mindset
- 10% is how you deal with life circumstances: car crashes, winning the lottery, death of a family member, getting a great job

What's amazing is that you can control almost half of your access to happiness. Our mindset comes from our actions, intentions, and habits. Sonja says, "Our intentional, effortful activities have a powerful effect on how happy we are, over and above the effect of set points; these are these generic things, and the circumstances we find ourselves in." We can actually work towards being happier!

We are going to build on this by discovering ways to access happiness directly from your relationship with your clothing.

Sounds crazy I know, but it works. Science proves it. First, let's see just how happy you are by taking a quiz.

How Happy Are You?

In the ReFashion Online Workshop, follow the link for [Happiness Survey].

In ReFashion Workshop we are using the PERMA Profiler to measure your well-being and happiness, so that as you delve deeper into the practices, you will have something to compare yourself to later. Consider it a first marking point.

Journal

1. What was your score on the PERMA test?

   a. Positive emotions =
   b. Engagement =
   c. Relationships =
   d. Meaning =
   e. Accomplishment =
   f. Health =
   g. Negative emotions =
   h. Loneliness =
   i. Overall well-being =

2. Reflect on a recent time when you desired a certain outfit or article of clothing that you later acquired. How long did the happiness last? How often do you purchase apparel to boost your happiness? Once a month? More? Write down the last five purchases you made and when they were made. Now write down why you made that purchase.
3. Contemplate your current state of well-being. What weak areas can you improve upon, moving forward?

4. Meditation: In a quiet place where you won't be disturbed, sit with your eyes closed for the duration of ten minutes. Breathe in naturally. Allow your mind to quiet down with each intake of air and each exhalation. Let it calm you and soothe you as you follow this sensation down your throat and into your heart. There, breathe large breaths, fully inhaling into your lungs until you feel the breadth of your chest expand larger naturally. Stay there, and let yourself feel what level of happiness you are at. Stay with it.

11

Jeans

They have expression, modesty, sex appeal, simplicity — all I hope for in my clothes. I wish I had invented blue jeans.

— Yves Saint Laurent, French couturier

I vividly remember growing up in Florida in the bustle of high school where everyone seemed to have more than I did. More clothes, more shoes, cooler backpacks, and noticeably nicer blue jeans. Coming from a family of seven with five kids, it wasn't particularly important to my mother for us to have name-brand clothes. We were frugal, so much so that at one point I had outgrown all of my jeans and earned the nickname "Highwaters," purely because I was too embarrassed to ask my mom for more. I would have sold my entire beanie baby collection for a pair of Levi's jeans. Instead, I thrifted at Salvation Army until I found cheap, worn-down Levi's that I tailored to become skinny jeans.

At that time in Jacksonville, there wasn't even a decent mall; and to everyone else tight denim was ahead of its time. Hilariously, given the muggy climate of Florida any time of the year, even when it was close to boiling outside, everyone could be seen wearing blue jeans. It was ubiquitous. It was a normal part of life. And that is the power of blue jeans. In America especially, they are a second skin.

Jeans represent all that is good, bad, and ugly in fashion. According to Bel Jacobs of Extinction Rebellion, to this day, blue jeans are the number-one type of apparel sold in America. Chances are, you are wearing jeans as you read this. And if not now, then tomorrow. Aside from socks and underwear, jeans are the most popular clothing to date.

Bel reports that 5 billion pairs are made every year, and that half the world's population is wearing jeans on any given day. Blue jeans are what the garment workers at Rana Plaza were sewing and inspecting when the building crashed down on them in April of 2013, killing 1134 workers and injuring another 2500 – the deadliest factory accident in known history.

According to Fashion Revolution, it takes a lot to produce blue jeans:

- 10,000 liters of water are required just to grow the 1 kilogram of cotton needed for one pair of jeans. To compare, that's how much water one person will drink over a span of ten years!
- One pair of 501 jeans produces 33.4 kg of carbon dioxide, which is equivalent to 69 miles driven by the average US car, or watching 246 hours of TV on a big plasma screen.
- Just the finishing process alone uses 18 gallons of water, 5 ounces of chemicals, and 1.5 kilowatts of energy. In total, that equals an astonishing 92 million gallons of water, 7.5 billion kilowatts of energy (enough to power the city of Munich for a year), and 750,000 tons of chemicals each year.
- The cotton required to make blue jeans is one of the biggest products in agriculture.

But there are safer and more sustainable ways to grow and harvest cotton that have less of an impact on the environment. I spoke with my longtime neighbor and member of the community in Venice Beach, Ryland Engelhart. Ryland is the founder of Kiss the Ground, a nonprofit that focuses on regenerative farming practices in the form of education and also in practice with their own farm-to-table restaurants Café Gratitude and Gracias Madre. Ryland has some fascinating ideas on how to change how we grow thirsty crops, and thus help to create a more sustainable cycle of agriculture for the betterment of the carbon cycle.

Exclusive Interview with Ryland Engelhart of Kiss the Ground

RE: "There are ways to grow plants in a manner that actually heals the planet, brings the carbon out of the atmosphere back into the ground, allows for more water to infiltrate into our aquifers, recharging them, recharging springs, allowing streams and rivers to come back, enhancing biodiversity, creating more nutrient-dense food, creating greater habitat for more than food production or for crops that we're harvesting, but also more environment for biodiversity and wildlife to also thrive inside of an agricultural system. For 1% increase of organic matter in soil, you can hold 1000 more gallons of water within that soil.

"Carbon is the building block of all things that are alive. And that carbon has come from us eating either green plants, or things that ate green plants that ultimately got that carbon from the atmosphere. When plants photosynthesize, they use the sun's energy. They pull carbon out of the atmosphere through little stomata on the bottom of their leaves. They sip that carbon in like straws, and they build their bodies. And then they send those carbon sugars, carbohydrates, carbon and hydrogen, carbon and water down into the roots. And they feed microorganisms that are the microbiome of the soil. If we increase just 1% of organic matter per acre, we can sequester somewhere between 3 and 10 tonnes of carbon per acre per year into our soils through regenerative agriculture.

"And, as they feed those microorganisms that carbon sugar, those microorganisms provide minerals and nutrients into those plants in those foods, until you have this exchange of nutrient density going between the soil and plants themselves. You have this exchange of the carbon feeding into the microorganisms, the biology of the soil, and that carbon then becomes stored in that soil.

"This 5-million-year-old technology that ultimately created the planet that we have today is because of the exchange of plants and microorganisms pulling carbon out of the atmosphere, and storing carbon into our soil. This process is what created a planet habitable for life. There's actually twice as much carbon in our soils, currently, as there is in the atmosphere. And there's actually a lot more room for more carbon in our soil that is ready to receive it if we, you know, we're stewarding land in a way that really acknowledges this bigger connection, bigger loop of the carbon cycle.

"Some of the principles of regenerative agriculture are called 'no till' or 'low till.' You can do it with any plant, and in the USA, we should be doing it with cotton. The idea is that you should not be tilling the soil every year because there's life in the soil. The soil is a network of a living system, a web of life. And when you till it, you essentially break that web of life. When the land is being tilled, you're exposing the soil to oxidation, to the elements; you're exposing the air, the sun, the wind to the biology in that soil. And when it's being exposed to the elements, a lot of living organisms die from oxidation and turn into carbon dioxide that is released into the air.

"When you're rotating a cover crop in the offseason for, let's say corn... Corn is a very nitrogen-intensive crop, it requires a lot of nitrogen to grow. So someone could cover the same land in the offseason when they're not growing corn with fava beans, legumes. Because legumes fix nitrogen out of the air, and they put that nitrogen back into the soil and help create fertility for that next crop of corn the following year.

"So, no till, cover cropping, focusing on biodiversity — meaning, you know, not a monoculture. Most small farms are a mix of all different kinds of crops. Large industrial farms generally are a monoculture, so they are only growing cotton on that land. One way to heal the soil is to create a diversity of plants being grown. Another distinction is planting perennial foods, like trees, and vines, and bushes, versus annuals, which are grains or vegetables where you plant a seed, it grows for a season, you harvest it, and you have to replant, fertilize, and grow the next year. Where a tree will give an apple or an olive or an avocado year after year with less disturbance to the soil, less need for fertility and fertilizer. And oftentimes, less water even.

"Then there is animal integration. One of the most successful ways we're regenerating land is through what's called adaptive or holistic planned grazing of animals where we're reintroducing animals back to grasslands, prairies, or pastures where the soil has been degraded. Actually, the grazing and the pooping and peeing and the movement of those animals has a sort of cycle on that land. Moving them from place to place, specifically, actually creates this enhancement of life and enhancement of forage, meaning more grass can grow year after year. You can have this regenerative effect. That's why in the prairies, in the Great Plains, when you had bison rotating over the prairie for millennia, you had 13 feet of topsoil. That topsoil was built by the integration of animals and grasses, and predators moving those animals around those grasslands in a roving rotation. Now we can kind of mimic that on a farm system by moving cows to different paddocks or plots of land, over a period of time."

You can learn more about how regenerative farming could be the solution for carbon capturing in Ryland's documentary [*Kiss the Ground*] narrated by Woody Harrelson, or simply visit his website to learn more.

It is beautiful to think that it is possible to tip the scales on our energy-hungry denim jeans to where they become a player in capturing carbon instead of emitting it. Doing all we can to nourish our topsoil should be a top priority for us, moving forward. Talk to the local farmers at your farmers' market; ask questions about how and why things are grown. Recommend this enriching documentary to as many people as you can. We stand a chance of slowing climate change, just with the dirt at our feet.

Let the beauty you love be all that you do. There are hundreds of ways to kneel and kiss the ground.
— Rumi

Your Old Jeans

We've spent a fair amount of time traveling the world of thought in this workbook. It's time for some action.

Take a look through your jeans drawer, and use fresh eyes to determine which pairs are no longer serving you. Is the fit off? Are they a little too damaged? No matter, set them aside. You are about to participate in upcycling!

Blue Jeans Go Green (BJGG) is a denim recycling program that turns your old rags into denim insulation. Through using this program, you guarantee that your fashion has-beens have a second life. BJGG accepts denim of all kinds: skirts; shirts; shorts; pants with stains, rips, tears; and even scraps. They prefer denim that is at least 90% cotton and are only accepting donations from the USA, but that doesn't mean you can't contribute if you live elsewhere.

Zappos allows you to ship for free with their prepaid labels; there is a short-link in the ReFashion Workshop online classroom to [Donate Your Jeans].

As a part of my gratitude for this crucial step, once Blue Jeans Go Green has received your donation, you will receive a voucher for $20 off a new pair of pants at Holding Court. Now that is a balanced give and take.

Accountability

The day you plan to donate, tell your accountability partner. Let them know that if they have jeans they want to get rid of, you can add them to your package or they can create their own.

12

Kids at Work

These are conditions that you would never approve of for yourself, or for your friends, so why do we approve of them for children who are making our clothes?

— Lotte Shuurman of Fair Wear

While wandering the multilevel maze that makes up the city of Varanasi, India, I glanced through open windows into many homes that doubled as workshops. I was surprised to see children as young as 6 years old working feverishly on a loom. Their hands were calloused, and they had a faraway look in their eyes. Upon seeing me, they rushed to invite me inside to look at hundreds of scarfs piled up in a corner. And I ended up buying one not because I needed it, though it was frigid outside, but because I felt in some way I needed to support these children. When I imagine my nieces and nephews subject to that kind of life so early on, it breaks my heart.

It seems like a world away to imagine that child labor is a thing of the present day. Child labor is illegal in most countries, but it still continues to be a problem in the world's poorest communities. Across the globe today, kids are at work, and fashion is a big offender.

According to UNICEF, "Current global estimates based on the International Labour Organization and the World Bank indicate that 168 million children aged 5 to 17 are engaged in child labour, many working in the garment industry to satisfy European and American demands."

Why is this happening? To put it mildly, the trend of cheap, fast fashion over the past 20 years has pressured brands to chase a lower bottom line at any cost. The strain for low-cost workers paves the way for manufacturers to seek out the least expensive labor possible — and children do not have stringent laws or unions to protect them. Many fashion labels are unaware they are hiring manufacturers with child workers to make their product because the international fashion complex is sprawling, and there is little transparency between third parties and fashion houses.

According to UNICEF:

Factory recruiters target impoverished families with the promise of caring for their daughters better than they can themselves. Parents are told their daughters will be given comfortable private accommodations, three healthy meals a day, a livable salary, opportunities for training and school, and a bonus payment at the end of the three-year period.

But their field research shows that, "In reality, they are working under appalling conditions that amount to modern day slavery and the worst forms of child labour."

Children are sought after because the strenuous labor of picking cotton and threading machinery requires nimble hands, and children come by that naturally. They are also easily controlled and manipulated, and taught to believe that this is the best they will get; meanwhile they lose out on the precious incubation time that is childhood.

Children forced to work under poor conditions in weaving factories alone suffer in so many ways:

- Work-related injuries
- Ruined vision from working long hours in low light
- Respiratory tract infections from thread dust
- Numerous body aches and pains, even deformed spines
- Malnutrition, made worse by the force-feeding of stimulants
- Verbal and physical abuse
- No education
- Minimum or no pay
- Some children may actually be sold by their parents to pay mounting bills and thus are permanently separated from their families

"152 million people are affected by child labor annually. That number has to come down. It has to," stated Fairtrade representative Kasi Martin.

In every part of the supply chain, you will find kids at work. From children picking cotton in Uzbekistan, to India where the threads are woven, all the way to Bangladesh where the garment is assembled. The cotton industry employs children to transfer pollen from one cotton flower to another while being exposed to pesticides.

An estimated 60% of yarn spinners in India were under the age of 18 when they were employed, many of them reporting to have been hired at 15 years old. In the cut-and-sew stage, a study from UNICEF says:

In garment factories, children perform diverse and often arduous tasks such as dyeing, sewing buttons, cutting and trimming threads, folding, moving and packing garments. In small workshops and home sites, children are put to work on intricate tasks such as embroidering, sequinning and smocking (making pleats).

One of the reasons it is so hard to combat child labor is that it is very tricky to track down. Most companies in the US and Europe who have their clothes manufactured in Southeast Asia have no idea who is actually making their garments, and there are no laws in place that enforce transparency.

Child labor is a symptom of the larger and even more complicated problem that is poverty. Having few options, parents will send their children somewhere because they cannot carry the burden of providing for them, and the system reaps the benefits.

I spoke with Lotte Schuurman at the Fair Wear Foundation and she said, "If parents have no education, they will end up in low-paid work; their children will be forced to work. They will miss out on their education, and they too will end up in low-paid work as adults. You need to get out of that vicious cycle of poverty to decline child labour."

How can we do it better?

Fair Wear Foundation has a list of over 120 brands that have signed on to uphold their code regarding child labor. This requires companies to go beyond the regular standards and conduct in-house audits of their manufacturer. Similar models can be found with the Fairtrade Label Organisation, the Global Organic Textile Standard, and the Ethical Trading Initiative.

Shuurman says, "There are practical steps that companies can take to rid their supply chains of child labor. Brands can start off by creating a supplier register. Fashion brands normally have 200 or more suppliers. You should start by knowing who your manufacturers are and visiting them. On these visits, brand representatives must watch out for signs that the factory could be subcontracting; they should be concerned if the factory does not have enough workers for the amount of T-shirts it produces."

Brands can also address their timeline constrictions, which often add pressure on the manufacturer. Schuurman says, "To meet tight deadlines or unanticipated orders, factories may subcontract without informing the buying companies. Sometimes that is enforced by the brand; it puts too much pressure on the factory." Companies can adjust their purchasing practices to lighten the load and ensure that the factories they have inspected fulfill their orders.

Most people can agree that child labor is a terrible practice because it causes great harm and suffering to the most innocent of us. This leads me to the Third Noble Truth of ReFashion — the end of suffering.

The Third Noble Truth of ReFashion: The End of Suffering

The First Noble Truth of ReFashion is that the planet is suffering. The Second Noble Truth of ReFashion is that the cause of suffering is desire for more, and feeling that we are not enough.

The Third Noble Truth of ReFashion is that the end of suffering begins by waking up from the trance of separation, the small sense of self, the body of fear, and connecting to the global self.

Look at how interconnected we all are — with social media showing us the daily lives of people across the globe, and the ability to travel anywhere, even space. Infrastructure is breaking down old barriers. Races are blending together and gender is moving more fluidly than ever.

The clothes we wear are almost all international. Tencel is a fiber grown in Australia, broken down in Austria, and woven in Los Angeles. It is a hyperconnected world. The planet is an organism, and we are all parts of the whole.

Ending suffering is, in part, separating from your old conditioned desires and embracing interconnectedness. By phasing out your ego-based desire, pride, and the delusion of separation, you are liberating your mind into a heightened sense of awareness. We are going to deconstruct this old conditioning, and build a new one.

In the "Innovation" chapter, you took the PERMA Profiler quiz online to determine your level of well-being and happiness. We pondered about how wealth, materialism, and getting good grades won't make you happy in the long run.

Now we are going to look at practices that you can implement in your daily life that will help boost happiness and recondition your relationship with interconnectedness.

Changing Your Relationship with Happiness

In a study at Yale, two different groups of people who identified themselves as either Happy or Unhappy were studied and asked a ton of questions. Both groups contained people of all racial backgrounds and income levels. What the researchers found to be the biggest determining factor separating the Happy people from the Unhappy people was their relationship with kindness — kind behaviors towards themselves and others. Happier people are motivated towards acts of kindness, recognize kind acts more often in public, and behave in a kinder way towards other people.

Simply thinking about kindness makes you happier! In another study, Yale students were tasked, once a week, with remembering and writing down one act of kindness they had done for another person in the past. At the beginning of their experiment, students took the PERMA Profiler test to measure their happiness at stasis. After one week of performing the task they took the PERMA Profiler once more, and results showed that just thinking about kind actions improved students' happiness by a full point!

Actually performing acts of kindness can improve your happiness by three to five points over time!

Acting out of altruism boosts your level of dopamine — the happy chemical — in your brain, and creates a positive feedback loop with the person you are helping. It is a win-win scenario for overall well-being, and has the habit of creating communities centered on love. Ancient philosophers coined this experience "ethical egoism," and it proves to be highly effective at boosting your happiness while making the world a more loving place to live. Performing acts of kindness is a strong tool to add to your ReFashion toolkit.

What's more, altruistic spending is shown to increase your happiness! Liz Dunn and Mike Norton in their book *Happy Money* conducted interviews with random people on the streets of several different countries and asked them to rate their happiness. Then they gave them $5 or $20, with the rule that they had to spend it either on themselves or on someone else sometime that day.

They asked the participants what they predicted would be the outcome, and most people assumed they would be happier if they had $20 and spent it on themselves. When they checked in with the participants later, they found something significant. Not only were the participants much happier that they had spent the money on someone else, but also it didn't matter how much money it was they spent. The difference between $5 and $20 had little effect.

Consider the facts that you have learned so far about the fashion industry. If you treat supporting sustainable fashion labels as paying it forward to the environment, and supporting ethical brands as paying garment workers a livable wage, it is highly likely that your happiness will increase — no matter how much you spend! This isn't philanthropy in its purest form, which would be giving without expectation of an exchange, but it is a fairer level of exchange. It is altruistic spending that participates in the global economy. Not a bad happiness hack and level-up for your reconditioning as a steward of the Earth.

Random Acts of Kindness

This week, aim to perform seven acts of kindness. You don't have to do them once a day; you can do them all in one day if you want! And they don't have to be over-the-top gestures, but can simply be helping a co-worker with a problem, giving a few dollars to a charity you believe in, or writing a "thank you" note. Keep track of all of them in your journal.

At the end of the week, take the PERMA test again, and record your new level of happiness in your journal.

Journal

1. Reflect: on your experience doing random acts of kindness. Do you feel happier? Do you feel more connected and aware of the world around you? What acts of kindness could you do with your fashion habits moving forward? Write down five.

2. Contemplate: You could change your personal story to say, "I am a kind person." And it would improve your overall happiness. Contemplate on what it would feel like to own kindness in your personal story.

3. Meditate: For ten minutes in a quiet place, sit down, clear your mind, close your eyes. Follow your breath as it slows down, and feel in your body what it is to be kind. Breathe into it. Imagine someone you really love. Now, picture their face in your mind. From deep within, send them loving-kindness. Feel it as an emotion. Say to them, "May you have peace." "May you have joy." "May you have love." Now imagine someone you have a difficult relationship with — maybe a relative, or a co-worker. Picture their face and say to them, "May you

have peace." "May you have joy." "May you have love." Finally, feel deep within yourself to the spirit within, and say to yourself, "May I have peace." "May I have joy." "May I have love." Let this fill you as a ball of light that shines directly onto your crown down into your heart.

13

Multinational Workforce

In our haste to have easy, inexpensive things, we can completely forget all the hands our belongings pass through to get to us.

My favorite basic denim button-up that I bundle up in to sip my coffee on chilly mornings was cultivated somewhere in the world as a crop, picked by hands, and sent to another country where it was threaded into yarn by another set of hands, then sent to yet another country where several more sets of hands cut, sewed, and finished it. When I bring my purchases home, this journey across the globe with all of its karmic energy is often forgotten as soon as the item gets folded and put into a drawer. It's normal to disconnect from what we don't immediately see.

Let me paint a picture of the kind of lifestyles my button-up passed through.

Picture this: Somewhere in the Global South, the breadwinner for a family cut my garment out of a roll of fabric. They have children that they care for and send to school, and also have aging parents whom they are now caretakers of. But the company they work for is constantly under constraints from higher-ups to lower the cost of manufacturing, thereby cutting into their income at regular intervals. The workload doesn't change, and now they work overtime with no guaranteed pay. They have to pick up another job to cover their family's needs, and quickly become indebted to the same company they work for. Now, they cannot quit. And they still cannot support the needs of their dependents. A startling amount of garment workers do not earn a living wage at their factories.

To get the specifics of the story of the garment worker, I woke up at 4 a.m. to call Lotte Schuurman of Fair Wear in Amsterdam. Fair Wear, as mentioned earlier, is an organization that looks over the welfare of garment workers globally, by partnering with over 140 brands who have agreed to let Fair Wear oversee factory floors and connect with NGOs and governments to ensure a safe workplace and a living wage.

Exclusive Interview with Lotte Schuurman of Fair Wear

CB: "Tell me about Fair Wear Foundation."

LS: "At Fair Wear Foundation, we work with garment brands and other brand influencers to improve labor conditions in the garment industry. In the past 20 years we have learned how to work with garment brands to better labor conditions. We know that brands have a huge influence on the labor conditions of factories, and we are working with brands determined to find a fair way to make their clothes. I think if you ask brands why they joined us and are still a member of Fair Wear, I think it has to do with the fact that we are focused on people. We are asking brands to make the people who make their products front and center. Also by joining us they are letting an independent organization check and monitor what they are doing to improve labor conditions. And that guarantees a level of credibility. It is better to let an independent organization say it for you. Plus more and more consumers are asking garment brands to open up about working conditions in their supply chains. At Fair Wear Foundation, we publicly report on how well our brands are doing. That guarantees a level of transparency that consumers can trust."

CB: "How are brands committing to change?"
LS: "Once they join Fair Wear they are committing to our eight labor standards throughout their whole supply chain. First of all, they need to know where they are producing. If you don't know, then you can't change anything. Then you need to know if they are subcontractors. Then what the conditions are on the factory floor, so then you can truly work towards better conditions. You can't leave it up to the factory. You have to collaborate with your factory. And you have to look at how things are going at your head office. Because brands may not pay the workers in the factory directly. That is what the managers are doing. But they do have a lot of influence on their purchasing practices — the way they set prices. They need to pay a fair price without putting the factory under pressure. It is also important that brands cooperate together. All brands deal with poor labor conditions. If we really want to make change, then all brands need to start working on better labor conditions together.

"We have been working with brands for over 20 years in 11 different countries. We have audit teams, training teams, and people who man our complaint helplines. So we hear a lot from workers about how things are going."

CB: "How is fair labor relevant to the fashion industry today?"
LS: "We find that American consumers spend a smaller part of their income on clothing. The spending of the total wallet has been cut in half since the 1990s. But there has been an increase in the number of units of apparel sold. So clothing has become cheaper. And that is happening while low wages and poor working conditions still hit the news on a regular basis.

"That is why it is super-important that we all work together to make sure garment workers make enough to cover their needs and their family's needs."

CB: "What is a favorite moment you've had while working with Fair Wear?"

LS: "When I visited Bangladesh I got to see with my own eyes what it's like to work at a garment factory. Talking to workers, trying to sew myself even. I joined a Fair Wear training that helps women workers and their managers to prevent violence and harassment — a very important theme at Fair Wear. I also observed a training for an anti-harassment training committee that was established in the same factory. On my last trip I joined a drawing workshop that I still think about, because workers were asked to draw their family and their work life. Emotions ran high. Many workers have very emotional stories. One of the women told us that she was 11 years old when she got married, and three years later she got pregnant. She talked to us about her violent husband who left her. She stays with her seven brothers and sisters, and her parents and her children in the village. And when we met her she had already worked in the garment factory for 14 years. And she was still responsible for all expenses for the entire family. It was a touching experience actually, to hear those stories and see where they work. And respect what they're doing."

CB: "Can you discuss the idea of a living wage?"

LS: "By definition, a living wage means workers are entitled to a wage they and their families can live on. In the Fair Wear 'Code of Labour Practices,' a living wage is defined as a wage paid for a standard working week that meets the basic needs of workers and their families and provides some discretionary income.

"Keeping in mind the local cost of living, a living wage covers:

- Clean water
- Nutritious food
- Shelter
- Clothing
- Education
- Health care and transport
- Discretionary income for unexpected expenses."

CB: "What about the workforce?"
LS: "In the past 15 years, the international garment industry has doubled to a workforce of 80 million strong, and while the explosion of easy-access fashion is a booming industry for retailers, it creates a lifestyle of deprivation for the vast majority of workers and their families.

"It still surprises a lot of people that expensive clothes are not necessarily better made than cheap clothes. It is a fact that fast-fashion brands and luxury brands can be made in the same factories by the same underpaid workers. Somewhere between 2–5% of what you pay for in the shop goes to labor costs.

"What you see is that brands pick up their business and go to other countries when wages go up. We see that happening in China, and then Bangladesh, and so many more. That's what's happening right now. On one hand you can imagine that governments are a bit reluctant to raise minimum wages because they want to keep the business. And that makes it very difficult. They need to economically profit from the garment industry, but workers need higher salaries; and for that to happen, brands need to pay their fair share."

CB: "How does minimum wage impact the workforce?"
LS: "What we see sometimes is that when minimum wages go up, many brands aren't able to pay their fair share, to pay a higher price. And that puts a factory in a very difficult position, that can even lead to closure.

"It's not always that brands don't want to pay more, or that they are evil or bad, but because, maybe, they don't know how to come to a fair price because the whole garment industry is not super-transparent. So if you negotiate with a factory about a price, it's usually a set price. They aren't transparent about which part of that price goes towards labor costs. It's what we call 'open costing.'"

CB: "How does this impact women?"
LS: "Overall the majority of the workforce we are talking about here are women, about 80%. Women in the Global South are often primary caregivers to both children and the elderly. This places an extra burden on women who also have multiple jobs to cover the cost of their entire family, while also implementing unpaid work of home care after hours. Her costs include food, rent, transportation, house supplies, school, emergency visits, and childcare when she is working overtime. There are discussions happening that encourage a gendered pay increase to help with this. But it would have to be implemented on an international level, in order to bypass regional societal norms.

"In Cambodia, it has been reported that women working in factories often only eat 1500 calories a day, and easily fall into debt unable to pay for their most basic needs. This is a problem beyond Asia alone; it is happening in European countries like Romania, Bulgaria, North Macedonia, and Albania. The highest difference between women and men is in India, where women can go 350 hours with unpaid work and men just 52. Many women choose to live within walking distance of work to cut the cost of transportation, while limiting their personal mobility. It is a major problem."

CB: "How could brands improve the conditions?"
LS: "Brands cannot change the supply chain on their own. They need other players as well. You need the factories, of course,

but you also need governments; you need unions. So if we want big change to happen, we need all industry leaders to stand up.

"If retailers were to pay an extra 3% to their factory workers, they could easily raise the price of their garment 3% higher without consumers complaining. Even more so if consumers knew the extra padding is going to the hands that made the outfit, not just the brand name. Which means, if brands wanted to pay their garment workers a living wage right now, they could. Labour Behind the Label noted that it would cost H&M only 1.9% of the $2 billion it made in 2016 to pay all its Cambodian workers the additional $78 per month they would need to achieve a living wage."

CB: "Where can we find you and your amazing data online?" LS: "Instagram, Facebook, and Twitter as Fair Wear."

And Now, an Experience

"What's on Your Back," version 1

When I think about how one in six people on the planet are employed in some way in the garment industry, I can't help but wonder how that might reveal itself to me physically close at hand, and I could get an idea of where these people are. So one night I had a group of friends over, and out of sheer curiosity I invented a game I call "What's on Your Back." Here is how you play.

1. With a group of four or more people (the more, the better), have everyone stand up and come together in the center of the room.

2. Choose one article of clothing you are wearing right now, and read the tag (or have a friend help you). Determine where the article of clothing was manufactured.

3. Now that you all know, separate into three groups based on the region your clothing was made in: Europe, Asia, and the Americas.

4. Note the differences in the size of groups. This is a representation of the percentage of garments made in various regions across the globe.

5. Dig deeper. Below is a series of charts that tell you the minimum wage for garment workers for several countries and regions, compared to the living wage it takes for a person to have a comfortable life.

6. Discuss the results among yourselves. Before today, were you aware that garment workers are being paid less than what they need to live a comfortable life? Would you pay more if you knew it would close the wage gap?

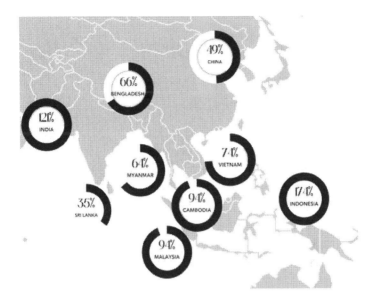

Circa 2022 data based on compiled charts from www. minimum-wage.org and www.tradeeconomics.com

Journal

1. Reflect on what you experienced during "What's on Your Back" and the reaction of your friends. Do you notice your community is in the dark about fast fashion and the harm it inflicts on human life? Were you surprised by their reactions? Were you surprised by the statistics? What did it make you feel about what's in your closet?

2. Contemplate the variety of clothes in your wardrobe. How much do you imagine was made in a country that does not pay a living wage to its garment workers? How does it make you feel?

3. Meditation: For ten minutes sit in a quiet place with your eyes closed. Breathe in naturally, letting it calm you with each breath. Follow your breath down your throat, into your chest; move with it as it goes down your arms,

and reaches your hands. Continue to concentrate on your hands, letting each breath empower sensation and fullness. Stay there. Your hands are tools with which you impact the world around you. Feel the power in them. What will you do with them this week? How can you use their sensitivity to heighten your awareness?

14

Naysayers

"Fashion is the second most polluting industry in the world" is the big claim, but what information is there to back it up?
— Many, many people I have met along my journey in eco fashion

In the quiet moments, following any lecture on sustainability I give — be it at the University of Georgia, Flagler College, or a runway show my brand is headlining — I notice a line of questions that always creep up from students and listeners. With sustainable fashion being such a new study, there isn't one place to go for all the facts, so within that darkness a space is created for a fair amount of naysaying.

According to Merriam-Webster's dictionary, a naysayer is "one who denies, refuses, opposes, or is skeptical or cynical about something."

To this day, I am surprised by how many people have not heard a single fact about the environmental and humanitarian crisis that the fashion industry has created. And while most people I encounter will be polite and not outright deny what facts I drop, I do get a decent amount of skepticism about how their habits make a difference at all. But as we know, they do.

For that reason, I collected the most common myths I have encountered around sustainable fashion, and I am giving you tools for how to talk with your friends in the future, and to feel more empowered to create a greener wardrobe on your own terms.

Myth 1: "You have to be wealthy to buy from sustainable fashion brands."

Think of it like this: You bought ten T-shirts that cost $10 each, and they all fell apart within a month. Compare that to one T-shirt that cost $40, but it's well made and lasts you for two years. Which scenario has the stronger environmental impact, and which one has the better impact on your wallet? There are many brands out there that are both quality and transparent *and* won't break the bank, and they will steer you away from fast-fashion impulse buys.

Myth 2: "People in developing countries will lose their jobs if I quit fast fashion."

Actually, fueling fast fashion only worsens conditions for garment workers in developing countries. And where there is space, something will always fill it. We have an ethical opportunity to shift the tide of the future of the industry and make room for jobs that pay a living wage.

Myth 3: "You need to commit 100% to sustainability, otherwise it doesn't make a difference."

This is not the case. No one is asking you to completely commit. As a matter of fact, if even 35% of consumers committed, or if you committed to 35% of your wardrobe being sustainable, it would cause what is called a "tipping point." A large minority has enough power to change the majority. We saw this tipping point happen in Hollywood with the #MeToo movement when females made up 35% of filmmakers, and all of a sudden the entire industry changed. Don't give up hope.

Myth 4: "Your wardrobe should contain only items from ethical and sustainable sources."

You've come this far, but if you have the urge to empty out your closet, please stop. The most sustainable piece of clothing you own is what is already in your wardrobe. As a matter of fact, if you wore your clothes just nine times longer it would lessen the impact on the environment by 20%. That is huge!

Myth 5: "You can buy as much as you like as long as it's from sustainable brands."

Even if you can afford to, buying only eco-brands doesn't give you a free pass to redo your closet every season. Remember, every purchase you make contributes to the impact on the environment. Whether it is organic cotton or regular cotton, there's no need for us to make so much of it that we each have 20–30 pairs of jeans in our closet. It's just not necessary.

Myth 6: "Sustainable brands can't be stylish."

While fashion brands might hold unique and timeless pieces that can fit many lifestyles, making them more ubiquitous, there are so many brands out there with bold prints and imaginative hues. But here's something to think about: Do you want to buy pieces that you are going to wear again and again? Our goal is to find clothes that suit our lifestyle and our own style language. And if you hold on to pieces and take care of them, there's a good chance that what you already have will cycle back into trend.

Meeting the challenge of your friends and community who might be naysayers is one thing. But there is a world stage that is complex and intermingled with multinational agreements and treaties, with each player holding their own agenda. It makes moving the needle forward very, very challenging.

One notable rebel who is at the head of the advance to reach naysayers within the government is Bel Jacobs of Extinction Rebellion. Known for extreme public civil disobedience, Extinction Rebellion has successfully blocked traffic on major bridges in London in protest against Parliament's actions towards climate change. They dug a hole in the ground in Parliament Square to represent the grave everyone will be in if we do not change our actions towards climate change. They have even used bike locks to bind themselves to the bars of Buckingham Palace, topless, with the words, "4 degrees C = Displacement, War, Starvation, Pandemic, Extinction," each painted across the bare-breasted chest of a woman.

Exclusive Interview with Bel Jacobs of Extinction Rebellion

CB: "What is Extinction Rebellion demanding from the governments of the world?"
BJ: "Number one, tell the truth. Number two, we demand net zero carbon emissions by 2025, which is incredibly ambitious. If we look at how reliant Western society is on fossil fuels, it's a big ask, but it's what we want. The UN is asking for 2030, but we are asking for 2025 because it is so urgent. The third one is convening People's Assemblies. The reason for that is, we want people to truly understand that we are in a climate emergency and to use their skills to turn this around."

CB: "What is a People's Assembly?"
BJ: "It is a group of people who are selected to reflect the demographic of the society you live in. Who will then come together in a room and will be presented with evidence. They

will come from all backgrounds, so you will have doctors, lawyers, but you will also have bricklayers and taxi drivers. Everyone has a certain expertise that you may not know about, and they will be presented with projects. So say they want to stop road building in Britain and look into all that it will entail. Experts will come in and say, 'This is what you need to do, this is how to do it sustainably.' And then they will thrash out what that will look like."

CB: "Has Parliament responded?"
BJ: "They did declare a climate emergency early on, and then immediately commissioned some major transport projects. I can't speak for all of Extinction Rebellion — we are such a massive decentralized group, we all work separately from each other — but under the common concern about raising awareness for the climate emergency, what we have noticed is the term 'climate change' has slowly been eased out with the term 'climate emergency.' Which may not sound like a big thing, yet to see the word 'emergency' works at a subtle level. Normalizing that it is a huge thing we need to get our heads around."

CB: "How are nonviolent demonstrations for the environment needed today?"
BJ: "At the start of Extinction Rebellion, Roger Hallam studied nonviolent protests as part of a course. And for me, I think it shows that the citizen and the ordinary person is becoming concerned enough to put their personal liberty at stake. When I joined Extinction Rebellion, I thought there is finally a group that reflects a degree of the panic that I feel about the climate emergency, and it gives me something to do. I cannot sign any more petitions because they seem to disappear. And I can't seem to reach my elected representatives effectively enough. And I just need to get out on the street as big as I can with a

group of people who believe in the same causes. So I think it's just a way of bringing attention to how urgent ordinary people think this problem is. We need to tackle it, and this is how we are going to do it. They always have to be nonviolent. They can be disruptive, as disruptive as possible, but they must be nonviolent."

CB: "Are there any common myths regarding civil disobedience?"
BJ: "I feel like a lot of people don't want to join Extinction Rebellion because they say, 'I don't want to get arrested.' There are still formats in place where you can still be a part of an action and not get arrested. If a police officer gives you direction of where you should stand, if you move to that area, you shouldn't get arrested. That is the biggest myth; the fear of being arrested stops people from getting involved."

CB: "Does a specific event that you have participated in stand out?"
BJ: "The funeral march that we held on the last day of London Fashion Week was particularly moving.We just walked down to the main event at London Fashion Week with three coffins representing people and the planet. It was really, really moving and stood out in that we tried to represent the concerns of the Global South as well in the speeches that we gave. There was a lot of grief in it. The basic response is that it was emotional."

CB: "Are there any emerging technologies that you are excited about?"
BJ: "Catherine Hamlet is one of the first fashion activists from the 1980s and she is very interested in hydrogen as a fuel. She says it doesn't emit carbon pollution like petrol does; it emits water vapor. I'm more keen on fashion technologies that can separate fabrics from each other. Someone's come up with a

technology to separate cotton and polyester blends so that you can recycle fabrics. But I would also say we need to plant trees to capture some of the carbon, and we need to reduce consumption everywhere."

CB: "Who do you recommend we buy fashion from?"
BJ: "Yvon Chouinard of Patagonia gave a really good talk recently; you should listen to it. It basically said that in about 20 years, high-street fashion won't exist anymore because we won't be able to create it sustainably at all. He is doing some really advanced stuff. Patagonia might be one.

"But I would say look for small local labels who are doing it right. They are trying to work with the Global South, so any label that is small that works with groups that need support, working as ethically as possible, should be on your list. Birdsong, Mayamiko, and a brand in Sweden called Asket."

CB: "Where can we connect with you online?"
BJ: "Instagram @Xrboycottfashion."

Pascal's Wager

Have you ever found yourself locked in a heated argument with a climate-change naysayer who just won't believe the science? It can be incredibly frustrating trying to discuss the irrefutable evidence of human impact on the planet with someone who just refuses to allow an inch of personal responsibility. Well, if they won't listen to science, maybe they will listen to philosophy. This little argument was built for naysayers. It forces them to choose a best-case scenario for their own personal well-being, instead of arguing about which scientist from which party said what.

The original argument created by Blaise Pascal (1623–62) was published posthumously in his book *Pensées*, and posits a wager for the existence of God. With the same structure, we are reimagining Pascal's Wager to determine our impact on the environment. In his work, he created a handy chart with four determining factors and four outcomes that show your possibility of infinite gain or infinite loss.

Pascal's Wager Reimagined

The Four Determining Factors Are:

A. You believe we are negatively impacting the environment.
B. You don't believe we are negatively impacting the environment.
C. We are actually negatively impacting the environment.
D. We are not actually negatively impacting the environment.

Imagine: A coin-toss game is being played where heads and tails are the truth of the environmental impact of fashion.

You, as the player, either believe you are negatively impacting the environment, or you don't.

- Heads: the fashion industry creates considerable damage on the environment
- Tails: it does not
- You toss the coin

The Four Outcomes Are:

1. A.D. You believe we are negatively impacting the environment, and we are not! = Infinite Gain
2. B.D. You don't believe we are negatively impacting the environment, and we are not! = Partial Gain
3. A.C. You believe we are negatively impacting the environment, and we are! = Partial Gain
4. B.C. You don't believe we are negatively impacting the environment, but we are! = Infinite Loss

You see, the infinite gain of positive results decreases as we get further down. The most positive being that you make choices to have a low environmental impact, and the inhabitants of the Earth are grateful, but are not in true danger. The middle tier considers the conscious consumer doing their best to have a low impact, because what you do does harm the environment.

Infinite loss happens at B.C., where you don't believe in your environmental impact, but it turns out to be true. You live your life actively polluting more than the average person, negatively impacting our planet and bringing it closer to an inhospitable habitat. If we had a world with nothing but B.C.s, we would be doomed.

We have a higher chance for a life of infinite gain if we choose to believe that we have an impact on the environment. Choosing to believe this ensures that we have a hospitable planet, even if it turns out not to be true. We live as if our impact could harm Earth, and make choices to preserve the planet's quality.

It is safer for our naysayers to wager that we are damaging the planet than not!

Journal

1. Reflect: Can you think of anyone who is a fast-fashion naysayer? Would this be a good argument for you to try on this person? Write down their name and how you would discuss this with them. It is important that we make an effort with even our most difficult acquaintances to see the other side of their ignorance.
2. Contemplate: Do you understand Pascal's Wager? How does it make you feel?
3. Meditate: For ten minutes practice the sensation of outreach. Find a quiet place where you won't be disturbed. Close your eyes and cross your legs. Let your breath slow

down naturally, focusing on the place behind your eyes, your prefrontal cortex, the region of your consciousness. While you are here, explore the sensation of opening up to places that are uncomfortable and pushing to a further largeness. Let your awareness grow larger than your body, larger than your room, larger than your house, larger than your city, larger than your state, larger than your country; let your conscious awareness grow as large as the whole world. Breathe here.

15

Oceans and Plastic

There will be more plastic in the ocean than fish by 2050, and more PPE in the oceans than fish by the end of the century.

— Adrian Grenier, actor-activist

I grew up surrounded by water. I am a Floridian, after all, and my favorite memories from high school are the days I played truant, skipping school to soak up the sun and sand at the beach. I reveled in the grayish blue of the salty, undulating waves. I threw myself into the ocean, every time with profound openness and joy. The oceans feel like they have different personalities. The Atlantic is a cheeky and playful woman. The Pacific is a bold and wise old man, dangerous. The Indian is sharp and young. With the minerals, the briny moist air, and the grand openness of it all, the ocean is my place of peace, my place of easily accessible bliss.

It is striking to consider that a force as powerful as the ocean, the movement of water that creates the very weather patterns of the planet, could be in danger. The particular danger here is the danger for the life inside it. The ocean has a surprisingly delicate balance of alkalinity and acidity, temperature, oxidation

— all the perfect recipe for the plants and animals living inside it to survive. Even a minuscule change in one of these ingredients spells disaster for the ecosystem. And in the age of humans, we are escalating things, per usual.

A friend of mine, actor and activist Adrian Grenier — founder of the Lonely Whale, a nonprofit that focuses on helping businesses and governments commit to protecting life in the ocean — came to mind when I wanted to know how the fashion industry and ocean degradation are connected. He hit me with rapid-fire facts about the state of our precious large bodies of water.

Exclusive Interview with Adrian Grenier

AG: "It's a problem with microplastics. Plastic particles washed off from products like our synthetic yoga clothes contribute up to 35% of the main plastic that is polluting our oceans. Every time we do our laundry, an average of 9 million microfibers are released into wastewater treatment plants that cannot filter them, and so they are released into the oceans.

"Not only are we drinking microplastic from our clothes — as water evaporates in the atmosphere it carries the plastic with it; we are breathing them too. Something like 13,000 to 68,000 plastic microfibers from our clothing, carpets, curtains, and other textiles are taken into our lungs per year. The consequences of this ubiquitous microfiber pollution seem clearly disastrous to animals and humans in both water and land.

"And of course it's all linked to poverty and people trying to survive. So that starts to open up an intersectionality on how all environmental degradation is linked to how we treat our own most vulnerable in our society. They are the ones who are going to pay the brunt of all of the environmental destruction. It all comes back to the same thing, which is, we all need to reconnect with ourselves, with each other, and the natural world."

CB: "How do you imagine we can change our relationship with the environment for the good, on a global scale?"
AG: "I see it from a couple different perspectives. There is an immediate, tactical, and imperative need to address some of the systems at play that are creating real damage in real time — often irreversible and irreparable. So we need to deploy tactics to prevent that at all costs. If possible stop it, delay it, within the system that exists today. So think Sea Shepherd, or stopping the pipeline, or living in a tree to save the forest. That kind of stuff, activism stuff. I think that certainly plays a role.

"And then there's sort of, where I'm operating from right now, the second part, which is to create new systems which would replace the old systems. New systems, new materials, PLA, any number of upcycled, recycled, change of supply chains, closed loop systems. Create new systems!

"And then there is a third tier, which is transforming ourselves from a human-to human-level — who are we, what do we dream of at night, what do we want to build for ourselves, what gives us deep satisfaction and fulfillment? So that it's not linked to the American Dream and capitalism. So that you can uncouple it from: 'I will be happy when I have stuff and things.'

"There's always going to be resistance to the other two things if the human being's well-being, or sense of self, is linked to the benefit of the previous systems. It's sort of the basis for what's going on with the white privilege or anti-racism movement, where it's not just about the system. It's about, 'Can we inspire people to look at themselves and how they benefit, and question whether or not this is who they are. Or can they change their value system and look at their privilege and reject that privilege for a deeper humanity base, in how they are connected to the world.'

"For me, Black Lives Matter, #MeToo, the environmental movement, they all have the same root in our fundamental identity: who we are and who we want to become. And I believe the solution will be a spiritual one ultimately. And once you transform that at the core of us, all of the other symptoms, all of those things just go away."

CB: "What can we do as a society to fix this problem?"
AG: "I personally would encourage us to not use the word 'save' because it's linked to our disconnect with nature, where we put ourselves above nature. Where we could imperialize, exploit, or have dominion over nature — or add concrete to control it, or control the seasons — all of the mechanisms so that we aren't a victim of the seemingly chaotic, unrelenting fear that we have of the unknown and death. So we order a bunch of concrete and we try to control it. This idea that now we need to 'save the Earth' is I think a continuation of that same mentality.

"Besides the first two things, which is to immediately stop all of the actions that we can. If we can do anything to allow for some relief, great. Don't buy fast fashion. Wear your underwear for ten years straight… haha. Any number of those things, okay, good. Create new systems. Work with sustainable companies, companies that are trying to do things differently. But then always come back to that third, which is what I think is the most important, which is to transform the way you approach the problem.

"There's so much arrogance in the environmental field. Everyone has an idea of what to do and they think they have the answers; meanwhile they turn around and are causing just as much destruction because they have blindspots. So, can you be as present, as sentient, as sensitive as possible; meaning you expand your awareness beyond your awareness of what you think you know. Find your own blindspots. I can't tell you how many ocean galas I've been to where they ask, 'Oh, would you like the salmon, sir, or would you like the tilapia?' 'Oysters on the half shell!' Not that everyone has to be vegan, but it's kind of undeniable that eating fish is problematic, knowing the stats. Eating meat is problematic, knowing how destructive that industry is, unless you are only absolutely buying from sustainable sources that you know for a fact. Then you have to question whether or not you really mean business.

"The way we approach the problem and the language we use, is it from a place of knowing? Is it from a place of arrogance? Or is it relenting and softening, and reintegrating with the parts of us that are wild and natural, and show some deference to the natural world, getting out of our conditioning of being in this capitalist culture. Do you really need to go shopping online today? Are we really going to self-isolate until we are lonely and disillusioned and go and create harm? A lot of the things we see with the violence are the same thing, it's destruction. Are we going to be more destructive, self-destructive, antisocial? Antisocial or anti-environmental. Or do we find that this communion with nature is so precious, so important, so life affirming that we want to double down on it. That we wouldn't want to do the things that would hurt things across the world. That we can feel so connected to it."

CB: "What are some tools you can use to reset yourself spiritually?"

AG: "I mean, it's as individual as the American Dream. I don't think there's one tool. But I think we have a collective opportunity right now to make those changes. COVID has given us all a break from ourselves, enough to perchance take a look at ourselves for just a moment before it comes rearing back in full gear and then we're in hypnosis again.

"Personally it's meditation; it's reading new ideas of new philosophies and borrowing from existing philosophies and spiritual, religious ideologies. I think all religions have a lot of wisdom to them as well. Then there's plant medicine. And I could give you a book list for myself, but maybe you don't even have to read, maybe you can just be predisposed to it. Some people are just born more awakened. Or their life experience has given them perspective enough.

"But it's also linguistic in nature. We're a very verbal-based, intellectual, science-based, egocentric society where we get stuck in our words and ideas as truth. We get so proud of ourselves that we can string a sentence together. And then we latch on to it; we argue with each other. And then there are panels on both sides of an argument on television. We see the world in this dichotomy. And it's really more challenging for a human to think in multilateral ways. I think it's practice, training, exploring, and those kinds of things. Also coming back into the body and the heart, the feeling space, and recognizing the truth of that. Because this is all projections and memories. They don't exist and haven't yet existed, and this is the only thing that is. And so, unless we are really feeling and being able to have a sensorial experience of 'what is,' how are we going to access the world and make decisions going forward? This is, I think, a coming home of sorts. Correcting our disconnect from our true nature, which is nature itself."

You can connect with Adrian Grenier at this nonprofit: www.lonelywhale.org

It is not a coincidence that our bodies are made up of 60–75% water, and our oceans cover 71% of the Earth's surface. The margin is very close. The balance and proportion of Earth and its creatures are perfectly done so that we can adapt and survive in our habitats. We are mirrors of our environment.

When it comes to water, it is clear that we need to change our programming for washing our clothes and caring for our waterways. And we are going to address that directly in the later chapter all about washing. But while we are here, we are going to improve upon our potential for happiness. If it makes us feel good, we will really want to be better stewards of the Earth!

One simple and easy practice you can incorporate to help you increase your happiness as you refashion your life is savoring. Savoring is the practice of stepping outside yourself to review and enjoy the moment. It forces you to notice and keep your attention here in the present, outside the default network. Attention is key to everything going on with you.

You begin to notice more when you savor. It also keeps you in the wonderful moment longer. I absolutely savor every moment I find myself at the ocean's shores or flying over breaking waves on a boat. Savoring makes a short moment feel like an eternity, and places a strong positive imprint in your mind. But you can savor more than just nature.

Here are a few activities you can do that will enhance savoring.

- Talk to another person about how good it felt.
- Look for other people to share it with.
- Think of how fortunate you are.
- Think about recounting this later with others.
- Show a physical expression of energy.
- Laugh or giggle.
- Tell yourself how proud you are.
- Be absorbed in the present moment.

Try some of these on for size when you feel like you want to slow things down and enjoy them.

The strongest tool we have for increasing happiness as planet healers is practicing gratitude, or rather the quality of being thankful and the tendency to show appreciation for what you have. Just thinking about how grateful you are has a powerful psychological effect that can redo your conditioning.

This is incredibly powerful stuff! Savoring moments in your life and sharing your gratitude can level up your happiness! And when applied to ReFashioning, these tools will increase other people's happiness as well.

Activities

1. You are going to practice savoring! Go to your closet and find five outfits that really speak to you, ones that have a special significance in your life. This could be a dress you wore to graduation, or something you wore on a special date. Think of memories that made you feel amazing and see if you can find the outfit you were wearing. Set them out on your bed where you can see them. Let your memory wander over the moments you had with those outfits. Consider doing some of the following.

   - Call a friend to tell them the story of what happened.
   - Think of how lucky a person you are to have had that experience.
   - Think about sharing this with a friend later.
   - Show a physical expression of energy! Put it on and wear it in front of a mirror!
   - Tell yourself how proud you are that that happened to you.
   - Be absorbed in the moment you are in now, and let this be a new moment to savor!

2. Gratitude: Make a list of five people, organizations, or think tanks that actively help slow ocean and waterway pollution. These could be your local government; it could be a science teacher from high school; it could be someone who has had an impact on you or your community. You can use the internet. Think about one

thing that you are grateful about associated with each entity on your list.

3. Choose one person or organization from the list above and share your gratitude with them in a letter. Handwritten is better if you cannot meet them in person. Thank them for their influence, and let them know their personal impact on you. Tell them what you are doing in ReFashion Workshop and what you are learning. Send it to them ASAP!

4. One step further. Show gratitude for your local waterways, a river, the ocean, a stream. Gather some friends or go on your own for a trash cleanup day. Group activities based around gratitude have been shown to increase your level of happiness even more; plus, you are doing something amazing for your community and for the planet.

Changes we can make:

a. Patagonia makes a product called Guppyfriend. This bag holds your synthetic clothes while in the washing machine, and catches the microfibers that would normally be washed away. So that you can just scoop them out and throw them away when you are done.

b. The Cora Ball catches fibers in the water while you wash, and has a fun spiral orb design.

c. Filtrol is a laundry-machine accessory that traps microfibers inside the discharge hose.

d. Finally, buying more plant-based apparel can, at the very least, change the type of microfiber we contribute to the environment. Plant-based fibers like cotton, hemp, bamboo, eucalyptus, and beechwood are naturally biodegradable and nontoxic. Consider the kind of waste you are contributing.

Journal

1. Reflect on the outfits you chose in the first activity. Write them down. What are they made of? How have you cared for them during the time you have owned them? How does it make you feel about your integrity regarding clean oceans and waterways? How can you fix this?
2. Contemplate how you feel after writing your letter of gratitude and after your trash cleanup day. Do you feel lighter? Do you feel more purposeful and complete? Would you do it again?
3. Meditate: Find a quiet place where you won't be disturbed. Sit down and close your eyes. Follow your breath in, all the way into your chest. There, feel inside for the gratitude you just felt after contemplation. Is it anywhere else in your body? Follow it there with breath, and let yourself be overcome by happiness.

16

Quality

Appreciate your clothing, appreciate what you have. Cherish it. What helps is knowing your own style so you don't have bad buys.

— Lotte Schuurman, Fair Wear

Whenever I get the itch to buy something new, I put to use a fun little trick. When I was working for BCBG as a model, they gave me so many luxury pieces, and I mean peacoats, gowns, chief-editor ready slacks, so many specific outfits that I had no practical use for. I started tucking them away in what I called my reserve wardrobe.

These were quality pieces, after all, even if some of them were very similar to things I already owned. I tucked them away into airtight boxes, and slid them under my bed where I would hopefully forget about them. My reserve wardrobe is where I went when I got bored of things I wore all the time. Because when you own luxury items, you cherish them, you don't want to just give them away; nor do you want to wear them all of the time — even if you have a full wardrobe of them.

The trick with the reserve wardrobe is to make yourself believe that what you just uncovered is something new to you.

It has maybe a few memories attached to it, but not many. And in many ways, it is new because you simply haven't worn it and identified with it in a long time.

Luxury items can get a bad rap, because as we have learned, sometimes the markup is just for the brand name alone. But sometimes the markup is, in fact, for craftsmanship, and so we need to spend a little time appreciating luxury fashion for what it is.

Nothing spells luxury quite like the red carpet of the Oscars. There is a movement happening in Hollywood that beautifully addresses sustainability in fashion and directly injects it into the heart of Hollywood's biggest event of the year.

Suzy Cameron, founder of Red Carpet Green Dress (RCGD Global), attended the Oscars with her husband, James Cameron, for his film *Avatar* in 2009. The film itself is a wonder, and happens to have a huge environmental message; and she decided she wanted to take the question of "Who are you wearing?" and flip it on its head. Instead she asked, "*What* are you wearing?" And very quickly, Red Carpet Green Dress — a contest that gives designers a chance to create an eco-friendly dress to be worn by a celebrity at the Oscars — was born.

Heading the charge at the RCGD nonprofit is Samata Pattinson, past winner of the competition and present creative director and chief of operations. She joined me in an interview for my podcast *Environmental Style Now*, and I asked her directly why we should care about luxury fashion in this day and age.

Exclusive Interview with Samata Pattinson of Red Carpet Green Dress

SP: "People are challenged by luxury fashion," she said, with her lilting British accent. "But for me, one of the things about luxury is that it's this kind of very rare, very beautiful, very considered, durable thing. It's usually handmade, something you treasure. It's not meant to be a throwaway item; it's not something you have to discard because it's poorly made. It's meant to be something you cherish. That is what luxury is to me.

"Durability is at the heart of sustainability, because we're looking for things that will last. We're looking for things that will not fall apart like fast fashion. I have so many passionate conversations about luxury fashion. People that understand the importance of it know that luxury fashion is its own market. Because of the pricing of luxury, it is sustainable as its own small ecosystem.

"I see luxury fashion as an art piece. Consider a gown. On a very purely artistic level, not a practical level, a gown is a design meant to inspire. And when you use that art piece for a bigger message, it creates a platform for conversation. I think when you actually look what we've kind of done with different gowns at Red Carpet Green Dress, whether it was the kind of vegetable-dyed fabrics Christian Siriano did for Daniel McDonald, or the kind of lab-made diamonds and crystals we use instead of conflict jewels, all of these are inspiration for how we can do things differently. The Red Carpet at the Oscars is a stage, and it is a platform like Louis Vuitton. You know, it's such an incredible luxury fashion institution.

"Somebody said to me once, 'Did you know that 90% of all the Porsches produced are still being driven?' I just thought that was so incredible, because to me, Porsches are obviously a luxury, luxury, luxury. That blew my mind. Because we couldn't say that about a lot of the fast-fashion pieces made today. That 90% of all T-shirts are still worn? No.

"But I think one of the things that frustrates me is, we have to understand that a lot of poor design in the fashion industry is strategic. This is not accidental. The fashion that we're buying, this inexpensive stuff that falls apart, is designed to do that. As somebody that used to be a designer myself, I know that you can design to be physically durable."

CB: "Tell me what it was like to win the Red Carpet Green Dress Contest."

SP: "I had taken a break from designing. I found the industry quite difficult and quite draining as a creative person with a business background. So I decided to stop designing for a while and reevaluate what I wanted to do. I always say about life, when you really want to do something, you can't get away from it. It's like that thing where you're like, 'Okay, I'm gonna think about this thing, I'm gonna think about music or fashion,' or whatever that passion is; and you try and step away from it. But everywhere you go, there it is! You turn around and there's this amazing billboard of this incredible gown, or every time you turn on the TV. So I couldn't get away.

"Ultimately, I opened up *Vogue* online and I saw a contest advertised, and I clicked on it. And what drew me in was it saying, 'Can you design a dress for the red carpet?' I didn't really read the second half of that sentence, which was with the sustainable twist. And that's when I said, 'Yeah, I can do this, I can design a dress.' And to me, at that point, it was just about materials that were sustainable. I didn't know about philosophy. I didn't know about anything else. And I just entered, and I shot my shot.

"And that's when, I think 11 days later, they called me and said, 'You've won this contest. So you've got to come to LA and make your dress.' And that's kind of how it all started. So really, it was a bit of a trip. It was really a trip."

CB: "I wanted to ask you if you've had a favorite moment during your time with Red Carpet Green Dress."

SP: "Being on the journey with Red Carpet Green Dress from the beginning, the CEO Suzy Cameron, wife of the famous director James Cameron, and I were going into meetings to try and convince people that this was going to be amazing. I found so much purpose working with her.

"We've had so many milestones together, so when she made me CEO, it just felt like the ultimate recognition of how much love I've poured into Red Carpet Green Dress. She opened up the stage for me to lead. As a woman of color, that was a profound experience. I mean, when you look at leadership, I think they say 12.5% of apparel companies on the Fortune 1000 list are led by women. Twelve percent! So to know that there's such little opportunity for women, and then I know that the same dynamics are echoed for women of color. When I was made CEO, it was a real highlight. I don't think it gets better than that."

Choosing Wisely

Luxury isn't exactly the enemy, then. From what Samata tells us, we can choose luxury pieces wisely and value them as heirloom pieces. The point is, doing it with mindfulness is how you will minimize all the negative effects on the environment we've gone over. We already know to look at the tag and see where it was made, and what it is made of, and we know to look for third-party verifications. What other tool can we use to choose wisely when we buy new clothes? I have a surprising answer I think you are going to love.

Remember that Character Strength Survey we took a few chapters back? Well, now we are going to use it to help you narrow down your personal style.

Martin Seligman in his book *Authentic Happiness* draws on your signature strengths to help you navigate through the material things you need for a fulfilled life. He defines your character strengths as: a desire, disposition to act, or a feeling that involves the exercise of judgment that leads to a recognizable instance of human flourishing. They are positive virtues that, when used, lead you to a happy and excellent life. Your character strengths are built-in, personal tools with which you navigate the world, and they are a superpower you can use to help you ReFashion your relationship with material needs.

Your character strengths tend to:

- Be ubiquitous among all cultures
- Be fulfilling
- Have a moral value
- Not diminish others
- Be the opposite of a negative trait
- Be measurable
- Be distinctive
- Be variable in all people

This led him to create a list of 24 Character Strengths, the same 24 from your VIA survey.

Of all the strengths listed, the ones that came out on top for you are the ones you exhibit the most, and also tend to be the ones that you value the most. These are called your signature strengths, or the character strengths that are most essential to who you are. How can you apply your signature strengths to ReFashioning?

Choosing Brands That Match

This is going to be good. You already know what your top five signature strengths are from the Character Strength Survey you took a few chapters back. We are going to hack your signature strengths to help you choose future fashion staples from brands that already have a strong commitment to environmental, social, and economic sustainability.

This is a very personal path. Not only will you get more fulfillment from wearing clothes that express your signature strengths, you will also discover new brands that are aligned with your intention to be a better steward of the planet. Also, shopping for your signature strengths will cultivate a hyper-focused style, which means you are less likely to return or discard your new clothes. This will lower your carbon footprint, and — according to these scientific studies — will give you more satisfaction and happiness.

1. Open up your journal to find the list of your top five personality characteristics from your Character Strength Survey. Take a moment to savor each trait that makes you you. Let it sink in how awesome you are. And imagine how your signature strengths translate into your personal style.

2. In the online ReFashion Workshop, follow the link to [Matchmaking] and browse our extensive list of eco-ethical shops. We have hats, shoes, dresses, bags — you name it — broken down into character traits and cost.

3. Search for brands that match your character traits. Go ahead and follow the links to see what their look is, and if it is something you vibe with. The point is to discover brands that match your personal style and are already doing what you wish to do — live as a steward of the planet by using resources that cause the least amount of damage.

4. There is no pressure to buy anything; as a matter of fact, don't. Not until you need something. But take a look at what is out there, and make a list of seven brands that kinda fit your profile.

Journal

1. Reflect on the results you matched with. Do you feel your signature strengths match your personal style? If not, were you able to determine new ones for yourself? How do you feel about fashion choices out there in the eco-ethical sector? Do you match well? Are there things that are missing?

2. Contemplate on what you feel will be your next fashion purchase. Is there an eco-ethical brand offering it? If it's not on the list, do your own search to see if it exists.

3. Meditate: In a quiet place where no one will interrupt you, sit cross-legged and close your eyes for ten minutes. Follow your breath into your nose and down into your lungs. Feel into your arms until you reach your hands. Breathe into your hands until they tingle and feel warm. This is a reiki technique, and it is very powerful for manifesting. Stay with your hands and the potential they offer you. After the meditation is over, notice how your hands feel different — more purposeful in daily life activity.

17

Recycle

Have you ever had an invitation you could not refuse?

I opened my phone blearily on the morning of my birthday. My room was chilly, damp, and smelled faintly of mold. It was northern Portugal and I knew special people were reaching out to me on my special day.

Scrolling through my Instagram chats I saw a message from someone I rarely, if ever, hear from. Someone I respect for his dedication to sustainability but also admire for his long and successful career as an actor. Expecting a birthday greeting, I was surprised to read an invitation "to a special opportunity I don't think you will want to miss."

Okay, you have my attention. He went on to tell me that a very select crew of people were invited to a party at Dracula's Castle in Transylvania for Halloween, hosted by a very famous founder of several household-name tech companies. He sent me the invitation and wow! Yes I wanted to go, and also, damn! How was I going to come up with the required costume of a fourteenth-century royal courtier with only five days of free time in a foreign country and practically no budget?

It was a three-hour scenic drive to Lisbon, where I set about scouring the city for beautiful embroidered end-of-roll fabrics, recycled poly satin, and anything from the thrift store that felt royal. My mind ran through what I knew of one-time-wear costumes most people buy for Halloween, and how people tend to just throw them away afterward; and I wanted to do something different. I wanted to make a statement by wearing home-sewn gowns to a one-percenter extravaganza, and I also wanted to participate in recycling because it is a well-known problem in the eco fashion corner of the world.

According to Fashion Revolution:

- 85% of all textiles go to the dump each year. The equivalent of one garbage truck full of clothes is burned or dumped in a landfill every second.
- Up to 95% of the textiles that are landfilled each year could be recycled.
- Only 1% of clothing is actually recycled.

Holding all of these fast-fashion facts in mind, I pieced together something I thought was beautiful, simple enough to sew directly onto my body the day of the party — since I didn't have a sewing machine — and easy enough to take apart after and reuse again for a completely new dress. You see, as a designer I'm not actually great at sewing. I have a sense of the origami it takes to drape fabrics and puzzle them together, but the actual sewing is something I've never studied. It goes to show that you don't actually need to know everything.

Nevertheless, once I arrived in my sparkling modern hotel room in Romania, I knew I had all the parts I needed to make something remarkable: the sheer beige fabric for my mythical Romanian Sânziene costume (the Sânziene are fairylike dancers of the woods who dance around bonfires under the stars), a hood and a crown of flowers, face painted black just below the eyeline like a mask in reverse, with ashen-painted hands. A little drape here, a little stretch there, cutting out a strip to make a cinch below the breast, folding and pinning fabric to make pleats with a safety pin, and then small precise stitches just where the fabric needed to hold things in place, and I had a dress that was shockingly complex to the naked eye, but startlingly simple. I was ready to see how it compared to the deep pockets I was about to mingle with.

To say this party was extravagant doesn't come close to what it was like to experience it. Overwhelming might be closer to the mark. Between the two main events, I was genuinely haunted by orcs, seated at a table with an Oscar-winning director, an Olympian, and several ambassadors for different nations. All while being surrounded by an overabundance of meticulously chosen bouquets, furs, a children's choir, dancing people in bear costumes, and the most elegant and eye-catching costumes I have ever seen. And I have been on a few red carpets.

Some of the guests had rented genuine 400-year-old pageantry from film houses in Hollywood; some had bought gowns that needed their own special suitcase to fit them in; some of them I know were custom made, and it showed. But after asking around, I was the only person there who had made my own outfit by hand and spent less than $100 on the entire weekend's worth of costumes. The genuine shock I was met with was worth it. Had I said nothing, no one would have been the wiser. For the more curious, I would pull back a piece of fabric and show where the precious few stitches were, and they just shook their heads not understanding how it could be done.

It can be done, affordably, and with just a little imagination. It's okay to make a few mistakes as you learn. It's most important to follow through. The compliments I got on my outfits gave me the perfect segue to discuss my cause of sustainable fashion. It was beautifully done and an easy conversation starter.

Even better, because the fabrics were almost entirely whole by the end of the night, when New Year's Eve rolled around and I was still traveling abroad, I pulled out the length of brilliant blue recycled poly satin I wore on the second night of the party, made one cut, and stitched myself into an entirely brand-new dress. Again people walked up to me to ask me who the designer was and were shocked to find it was sewn on with just a few precious stitches.

I was able to use the same loose fabric three times to make dresses that would have otherwise been a one-time wear. Hell, I still have that fabric in my suitcase and could make version four if I wanted to. The beauty is that when you allow a little creativity and choose to stay true to recycling and reusing what you already have, real magic can happen. You don't have to add your one-offs to the landfill just because the holiday is over.

Make a conscious choice like I did to slow your habit of buying one-off clothes and instead choose something versatile — even for costumes — that you can use again. Better yet, you can recycle old clothes back into your own wardrobe. As we know, it is actually very hard to truly recycle apparel at a facility. Let's smooth out these bad habits and get you closer to recycling, revamping, and reusing what you already own.

Sekhmet's Threads

Some of your bad habits could be more ingrained than you realize. When we repeat the same action again and again, it signals our brains to create pathways that allow for that thought or action to be carried out more easily. Basically, our thoughts travel down well-worn superhighways in our brains. When we want to change a habit, we must create deviations from that pattern in order to form new paths. This process is called neuroplasticity. It is one of the reasons why it can be so challenging to start those New Year's resolutions. Breaking the pattern means forming new patterns, real, physical patterns. And one of the keys to changing is discovering where your patterns show up in your life.

One way the ancient Egyptians kept track of their habits was by using a practice of knot tying. The followers of the lioness goddess Sekhmet were devotees of change, and — for them — transformation happened in the belly of Sekhmet. They would carry a string of hemp with them wherever they went and tie a knot into the thread whenever a thought or action occurred that they wanted to transform. Tying the knot was a physical action that signaled the need to do a counteraction to undo the bad habit. It was also a way of keeping track of progress. Once the string was filled with knots, they would burn it in an all-consuming fire as an act of devotion symbolizing the lioness Sekhmet devouring her offering. Transformation happens in the belly of the goddess.

Sekhmet was considered the protector of Divine Order, calling all things into balance. Sekhmet's Threads teach us to transform our weaknesses into power. The Egyptians would carry Sekhmet's Thread with them until they were certain of their transformation.

We are going to take an alchemical journey with Sekhmet through the ancient practice of tying knots. There is incredible power in walking through life with an honest symbol of your journey towards inner integrity with the planet and its people.

Practice

1. Measure out 12–18 inches of natural hemp. Sit in contemplation, reflect over your life, and choose a moment when you took up an unhealthy fashion pattern. It could be simply buying all of your clothes from a fast-fashion website, how you care for your clothes, or how you throw them away.

2. Focus on the first time you can remember taking up the pattern, what that felt like, and its end result. Now imagine an action that can take its place, one that is

better for people and the environment. Tie a knot in your string. You are giving this habit to Sekhmet to transform you, putting you back into the seat of your integrity.

3. Sit in thought for five minutes. Let yourself remember more times you acted out of unawareness or haste and contributed to the miscare of our planet and its people with your fashion habits. Tie a knot for each memory, and replace the memory with an action you can do moving forward. You can do this until you can't think of anything else to add.

4. Take this string with you for a week and track your habits. Are you tempted by ads on social media? Tie a knot. Are you about to wash laundry without using a guppy bag? Tie a knot. And remember to replace that thought with one of the actions we have mentioned before.

Journal

1. Reflect on how your week went. What kept coming up? What snuck by you? Was it easy? Write down five habits you noticed and transformed using Sekhmet's Threads.

2. Contemplate how you feel about your personal power right now. Do you feel your will is weak? Is it strong? Sit with yourself for a few moments and find out where you are. Consider how transforming your heart, mind, and soul into one that protects the planet and its people can enhance your confidence. Inner integrity is a superpower that we often forget about. Once you are walking in your commitments, once you no longer need to tie knots in Sekhmet's Threads, you will have an inner knowing that you are living in love. Caring for the planet is most certainly a form of love. Let no one tell you otherwise. No one can touch this.

3. Meditate: Find a quiet place where no one will disturb you, sit down with your legs crossed, and close your eyes for ten minutes. Fall into a rhythm with your breath. Clear your mind of thoughts and worries and follow your breath as it lulls you into a pattern. Let it take you to your stomach and stay there. Breathe into your stomach and feel your personal power. The feeling grows stronger and tingles your fingers and toes. Let it rise up through your chest, into your throat, behind your eyes, and above your crown until it surrounds you. Surround yourself with your inner power. Imagine a bright golden orb that no one can touch. You are protected and you are strong.

18

Synthetic

Polyester right now accounts for 60% of fibers that are produced every year. And that is a lot.
— Tara St. James, professor at Fashion Institute of Technology, New York City

I'd been living out of my car for three months — it wasn't the first time this had happened — when I booked the featured role in a Super Bowl commercial. Even at the casting call, I parked my well-worn CRV with coats and dresses hanging in the window, a hundred random bags of art supplies, keyboards, clothing patterns of whatever I was into at the time, and a full suitcase in the trunk, praying I wouldn't run into a casting director in the parking lot. During that period I'd often sleep on friends' couches or watch someone's cat while they were out of town. I lived on a boat for a time, and in an attic at a kibbutz in Silver Lake. Occasionally I got desperate and slept in my car in the Hollywood Hills and waved "good morning" to celebrities walking their dogs in the early fog. During those "adventures" as I would call them, most of my stuff, my closet, was boxed up in storage at a rented unit or some friend's house.

When I got the check from the commercial, I rented a cute 1920s bungalow in Los Feliz, and everything I owned arrived all at once in a big truck. It was better than Christmas Day. I started unboxing and cherishing every little thing that came out. It was right as I began my deep dive into sustainable fashion, and now armed with the knowledge of synthetic fibers, I was shocked to discover how much of it I owned. T-shirts, dresses, yoga pants, fleece jackets, blouses, leggings, stockings, stretchy jeans, socks, underwear... Growing frustrated, I started reading the tags for everything and throwing all the synthetics into a corner.

My wrinkle- and shrink-resistant polyesters, nylons, and acrylics made a small mountain. I was embarrassed to call myself an eco fashion advocate with *this* in my house. Why exactly were my synthetics a problem? Well, to cut to the chase, most synthetics are made from fossil fuel polymers.

According to the RSA:

- Polyester production is responsible for 700 million tonnes of CO_2, the equivalent of the annual carbon emissions of Germany.
- Once plastics are created, they're difficult to get rid of — only a tiny proportion of synthetic fibers are recycled, 1%, with most being landfilled or incinerated.
- Fast fashion is awash with new plastics — with as much as 88% of recently listed items containing new plastics on some websites.
- It can take between 250 and 1000 years for plastic to disintegrate. The jury is still out since it has been around for less than a century.
- With every wash, hundreds of thousands of microfibers are released into the environment — a 6 kg wash could produce up to 700,000 fibers.

When you think about it, petroleum is just really ancient plants that have decayed. What an amazing magical substance it is! Fantastic plastic has in so many ways improved our lives. Look at how we use it in hospitals and in space travel. But the problem is that because it takes centuries to decay, it is not a renewable resource. We can't rely on it. Synthetics have been the rage for more than 50 years and now comprise roughly two-thirds of fabrics made today. They clothe most of the population of the planet. But it can't last forever, and it is doing critical harm to the environment. Oil spills and fracking come to mind.

It is highly possible that thousands of years from now, when the humans of the future dig down into the earth to look at the fossil record, this very moment we are alive will have a line of demarcation made entirely of plastic. That will be our century's lasting mark. Plastic.

But I want to flip the conversation here because I learned recently that there is a product that stands a strong chance of replacing plastic; maybe not in my lifetime, but maybe in yours. The product is ancient, it's actually one of the Big Five Fabrics of antiquity, and it's insanely versatile. I am talking about hemp.

I had the pleasure of meeting Professor and Attorney Courtney Moran in Joshua Tree, California, who is a lobbyist for hemp with Agricultural Hemp Solutions. Over a cup of coffee on a sunny day, I asked her about the benefits of hemp and what is happening in the United States to promote its use.

"It is crazy what you can make with hemp," she smiled emphatically. "You can make fuel, biodiesel, ethanol, you can produce batteries. You can make biocomposites, you can make construction materials. Of course, textiles and clothing. You can make soaps, you can make food, you can make pretty much anything that you can imagine. There's still research that needs to be done about load bearing and other specifications for different products. But it's really incredible what can be done. I mean, I look around my home even, you know. I have sheets and blankets. I have clothes. I have soap. I have food. My car has biocomposites of hemp in it. So it's just that it really can be a part of everyday life. And that was actually a really big thing and something that had been studied by USDA at the turn of the century in 1914 before all cannabis products were boycotted."

"One day they will call it 'The Tree of Life,'" I quipped.

"I'm going to use that in class!" she laughed. "That's too good. But seriously, it's crazy that it just shut down. I mean, what are some common myths about hemp versus marijuana for people who just don't even know the difference? What's really distinguished under federal law is a THC concentration. The psychoactive or intoxicating compound found within the plant, the variety of tetrahydrocannabinol, is what the current law is based on. Hemp traditionally is non-intoxicating cannabis."

"So what happened after 1914 to shut it down?" I asked.

"Well," she said, "it was a slow process, really over almost two decades, three decades. But in 1937, the Marijuana Tax Act was put in place. What that did was levy a tax on different activities regarding *Cannabis sativa*. And there were different levels of taxes put forward. It was just another hurdle for farmers. It was burdensome. It wasn't really intended to create hurdles for true industrial or true medical cannabis use. But the effect was really just kind of, like a blanket prohibition against the cultivation of any cannabis domestically.

"When that happened, public perception started changing. We entered the *Reefer Madness* era; the movie *Reefer Madness* came out, which was really a campaign to instill fear among those consuming cannabis or thinking that they're going to. It was different, not only legislation that was creating hurdles, but public media that were creating issues and a whole new view around this point."

"Wild." I sipped my coffee. "Now that you have helped change the laws in the US to legalize hemp again, what do you think the environmental impact will be if we start growing it on a mass scale?"

"Oh, I think it will be incredible! Of course, you know, I think what we're expecting to see is that farmers will start growing hemp in rotation with other crops. And so it won't be replacing, it'll be supplementing. And when it's grown, it can remediate soil, meaning pull up toxins out of the soil; it can aerate the soil and provide a lot of different benefits. It is an excellent carbon-capture crop: 1 hectare of industrial hemp can absorb 15 tonnes of CO_2 per hectare. That is more efficient than agroforestry.

"We can make biochar, which is also very helpful for the environment. If a farmer starts doing that, and especially with certain different crops, they can get higher yields after they grow it in one season. Farmers will use less pesticides, less fertilizers, just depending on what they're growing.

"I think we'll see a transformation if, and when, farmers do start using it in rotation. Right now, I think we're still in our infancy. And since 2014, image reproduction has been around cannabinoids like THC. And a lot of cannabinoid production is more horticulture than agriculture. But as we start to see more infrastructure for grain and fiber being built and developed around the country, then more farmers will start growing it — and actually not only grow it just because they want to grow hemp — growing it in rotation with their other existing commodity crops.

"They're going to see how beneficial it is for their existing cash crop. You know, I think a very beautiful world is just around the corner."

You can find out more about Courtney Moran's cause for cannabis at her several entities:

www.agriculturalhempsolutions.com;

www.oregonhempfarmers.com;

www.Earthlawllc.com.

After talking with Courtney I found myself smiling for days when I thought about the future. Maybe we can replace fantastic plastic with a carbon-capture renewable fiber. Wouldn't that just be the solution to everything! Imagine wearing fresh hemp every day instead of wearing what could realistically be called pre-Jurassic black sludge.

How much more vital life-force does a plant fiber that has been alive in your lifetime have, as compared to an ancient molecule that was pulled up from the depths of the Earth? Energetically, you can bet the molecules closer to life are more potent.

Now that we know there is a solution to most of our plastic problems, I'd be curious to know how far *you* have to go to replace your synthetic fabrics like I did all those years ago when I was unboxing my wardrobe. So let's take inventory. In the chapter "Multinational Workforce" I introduced the game "What's on Your Back" to help give you and your friends a visual regarding where your clothes were made. Now we are going to do the same thing, but this time we are going to take a look at *what* your clothes are made of! Again, this is a powerful visualization tool and a way to break the ice with friends on what you have been learning in ReFashion Workshop.

"What's on Your Back," version 2

1. The next time you are with a group of friends, call their attention for a few minutes for a little experience.
2. With a group of four or more people, have them stand together in the center of the room.
3. Choose one article of clothing you are wearing and read the tag (or have a friend help you). Determine what the article of clothing is made of.
4. Now that you all know, separate into six groups based on the material your clothing was made of. Note the

differences in the size of groups. This is a representation of the percentage of each garment that is in circulation.

A GUIDE TO CLOTHING FABRICS

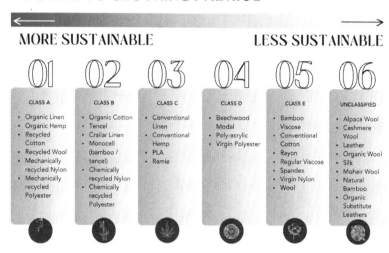

← MORE SUSTAINABLE   LESS SUSTAINABLE →

01	02	03	04	05	06
CLASS A	**CLASS B**	**CLASS C**	**CLASS D**	**CLASS E**	**UNCLASSIFIED**
• Organic Linen	• Organic Cotton	• Conventional Linen	• Beachwood Modal	• Bamboo Viscose	• Alpaca Wool
• Organic Hemp	• Tencel	• Conventional Hemp	• Poly-acrylic	• Conventional Cotton	• Cashmere Wool
• Recycled Cotton	• Crailar Linen	• PLA	• Virgin Polyester	• Rayon	• Leather
• Recycled Wool	• Monocell (bamboo / tencel)	• Ramie		• Regular Viscose	• Organic Wool
• Mechanically recycled Nylon	• Chemically recycled Nylon			• Spandex	• Silk
• Mechanically recycled Polyester	• Chemically recycled Polyester			• Virgin Nylon	• Mohair Wool
				• Wool	• Natural Bamboo
					• Organic Substitute Leathers

The Made-By Environmental Benchmark for Fibers is a guide that compares the environmental impact of the most commonly used fabrics in the garment industry. Its purpose is to encourage the adoption of sustainable practices in the fashion industry.

Made-By is a not-for-profit organization dedicated to promoting sustainable fashion. The benchmark ranks 28 different sustainable and regular fibers according to six criteria: greenhouse gas emissions, human toxicity, eco-toxicity, energy, land, and water.

Each fiber type is given a score, with the highest-scoring materials ranked as A grade. These include organic hemp, recycled cotton, mechanically recycled nylon or polyester, organic wool, and organic linen. E-grade fibers are viewed as the least sustainable in this clothing fabric guide. It's recommended to avoid these where possible and opt for higher-scoring alternatives.

Several fiber types have been ranked as "unclassified" because there was not enough data available when the classification system was run.

It's important to note that the entire life-cycle of a fabric is taken into consideration when ranking the fibers. For example, virgin polyester is energy intensive to create and made from nonrenewable resources like oil. It also sheds microplastics and does not biodegrade. On the other hand, conventional cotton requires huge amounts of water, taking up precious resources in often drought-prone areas. It also requires vast amounts of pesticides that are harmful to the environment and the health of farmers.

Overall, conventional cotton has a wider impact across human toxicity, eco-toxicity, land, and water.

Journal

1. Reflect: Make a note in your journal about the experience of "What's on Your Back," and consider what you could do to help improve your classification. How many people fell into Class E? How many were in Class A?

2. Contemplate: What percentage of your closet is a C grade or less?

3. Meditation: Find a quiet place where you won't be disturbed. Cross your legs and close your eyes for ten minutes, letting your breath guide you. Breathe easily, naturally, letting yourself relax. Empty your mind of any thoughts, and watch closely at what kinds of thoughts occur when they do come up. What are your repeating thoughts? Don't judge, just watch them. When you are finished, contemplate on how you can replace those thoughts with thoughts that will improve your happiness.

19

Toxicity

All toxic chemicals will affect your resilience; it's just a matter of what degree, or how long, or how quickly your body can recover from it.
— Dr Sam Shay, creator of "The Ten Pillars of Health"

Back in the dusty dry desert that hosts the Burning Man festival, fondly named The Playa, I returned for a second day to listen to biohacking expert Dr Sam Shay in the thankful shade of a covered dome. This was day two of a three-day lecture series, and after his presentation, sweaty but enthralled, I quickly dominated the Q&A to the point where he agreed to set aside time to talk about biohacking, particularly toxicity and apparel, where we wouldn't have any distractions. I can be very persistent, you see.

So we met at a remarkably posh watermelon-themed camp two days later, me dressed in a glitter bralette and a tutu and him wearing full war paint, an hour before he was scheduled to fight hand-to-hand combat in the Thunderdome. This is Burning Man — you can have life-altering moments of wit while dressed up like Mad Max. It was a challenge at first glance to take him seriously, until he started dropping facts.

"Whatever goes on you goes in you through the skin," he said, declining a slice of watermelon to keep his face paint crisp. "The idea that what touches your skin is a permanent barrier is a total farce. Because things are absorbed through the skin. There are all kinds of weird chemicals, dyes and solvents, and flame retardants on fabrics. The classic example is the huge amount of flame retardants people have in their bloodstream after they've flown in an airplane because of all the chemicals sprayed on the seats. No one is gnawing on the seat cushion as far as I know. So, it gets in through the skin. On subtler and grosser levels, it happens on smaller levels with fabrics.

"Once absorbed through the skin, it gets into the lymphatic channels and is dumped right into the liver. Sometimes it can go directly into the bloodstream, depending on how potent the chemical is that is worming its way through the skin. Your liver gets preoccupied in dealing with this new toxic thing that has never existed there before. So your liver has to now make some choices to prioritize its resources. Is it going to deal with this toxic chemical or is it going to deal with the hundreds of functions it's supposed to deal with?

"When your body gets exposed to these toxins it either has the capacity to deal with it, either in the short term or long term, or the liver can't deal with it and it causes damage. The term we are looking for here is allostatic load, which is the sum total of all of the negative inputs into our system until it hits its threshold and then we get symptoms or disease phase. So whether it is a mental stressor, or a physical energy, or emotional, or a toxin, all of those add to the allostatic load.

"You can have 100 people wearing the exact same clothing, and X number of people don't feel like anything is happening. X number may feel they have nothing happening, but they might get sick a day early, come winter. For the vast majority of people it remains an unseen contributor to their resilience, except for those canaries in the coal mine: the multiple chemical sensitivity types.

"When we wear something that is on us at all times, it off-gasses, and the chemicals that are in it, including what you used to wash it, it just weakens the body. No different from chronic sleep deprivation weakens the body, the same way toxic foods weaken the body."

I put down my watermelon martini. "Are there any toxins that jump to mind that I should be aware of? Aside from firefighter outfits?"

"That new clothing smell in wrinkle-free fabric? Are you familiar?" he asked. "That is actually urea resins and formaldehyde. Highly toxic. Also it's been estimated that a quarter of insecticides we use globally are used for cotton. Cotton is a super-heavy crop in terms of its use of fertilizers and insecticides. It's not benign. Watch out for regular cotton. In terms of synthetics, there can be a lot of petrochemicals in there. Petrochemicals are your nylon, acrylic, polyester, and they are toxic to the human body. There are also chemicals that are sprayed to prevent mildew or mold."

I coughed. "You are naming 95% of what people wear right now, you know that? What do you recommend is safe to put on our bodies?"

"Make as much shit out of bamboo as possible," he smiled. "Bamboo is a weed on steroids, it just grows, and grows, and grows. And it's antimicrobial and it can be soft. There are a few wonder plants that are great for clothing, and it would be very cool to see something made from coconut shells, since we have so much from everyone using coconut oil. But I would say bamboo is the single most sustainable fabric out there."

"While I have you," I said, "where can we find you online so people can find out more about your methods of biohacking?"

"For a free ebook on the Ten Pillars of Health, text 'biohacker' to 333–444 and put in your email, and you will be sent that ebook." www.drsamshay.com

And he was off to the Thunderdome...

What Dr Sam Shay had to share stuck with me. I was looking skeptically at my nylon tutu and sparkling bralette that was definitely smudging a glittery substance onto my skin, but I also no longer looked at plain cotton T-shirts as being so innocent anymore either. Like he said, a simple solution would be to wear only organic, non-Roundup-pesticide-sprayed fabrics. But if you are starting to feel a little fatigued with what you have been learning, buying, and what you already own, let's take a few minutes to remember that fashion can also be your ally.

- Style isn't working against you. It doesn't define you. You define your style.
- To reset your personal style, you need to shift your understanding of investing in the future and not just buy for the present. We invest today in what we pay for tomorrow. The health of our planet later depends on what we do right now.
- When you remember that using your money for good actually makes you happier, it's easier to choose sustainability and ethics over convenience.
- Awareness can change any energy pattern at will; you are a master of your own mind and can change yourself from the inside out with reflection, contemplation, and meditation.
- Personal integrity is a superpower that no one can touch.
- You are inextricably intertwined with the environment. As you love yourself, so love your neighbors and your planet.
- Use your influence for an altruistic cause.
- The planet and its people are suffering, and you have a part to play in the well-being of all things.
- The pursuit of material things is scientifically shown to decrease happiness.
- Acts of kindness, savoring, acts of gratitude, altruistic spending, and using your signature strengths are scientifically shown to increase happiness.

- The cause of the planet's suffering is our unhealthy relationship with base desires, which can be improved upon with awareness and reconditioning.
- If you are walking in the fullness of your kindness and compassion for all living things, then fashion is your ally.

Invisible Factors That Might Deter You

1. **Unpredictability:** Your life changes suddenly and you cannot fulfill your commitments. Jobs, relationships, house and home, finances — these could all come between you and ReFashioning.
2. **Disorder/Confusion:** You may not understand the deeper connection between you and your relationship with material things and miss the larger picture of the potential life you could lead.
3. **Convenience/Laziness:** You may begin to ReFashion your life, but then you allow fatigue to set in and fall back into your former conditioning, thus losing the opportunity to walk through life in a more aware state.
4. **Opposition:** Your change in habits may threaten someone else's worldview, and in order not to offend them or cause disorder, you succumb to erosion instead of evolving.

Making Fashion Your Ally

1. Continue to journal regularly about the fashion practices that evolve your happiness using reflection and contemplation, and finish with ten minutes of meditation.
2. Make changes in your wardrobe gradually, with focus.
3. Set up a lifespan plan for your apparel. How will you care for your clothes and how will you discard them?

4. Meditate in the mornings and evenings to promote the growth of gray matter in your brain and keep a clear mind throughout the day.

5. Take yourself out of peer groups and programs that tempt you to be an idle consumer.

6. Take your time when you shop; don't rush. Savor the moment and only buy what you need.

7. Use Sekhmet's Threads when you feel tempted to indulge your old habits. Transform your old thoughts in the belly of the goddess into new actions that empower you to be a steward of the Earth.

8. Choose experiences to replace compulsive online shopping; it will make you happier.

9. Send gratitude to people and organizations leading the fight against fast fashion.

10. Commit more random acts of kindness for your neighborhood and community.

11. Know what you need next in your wardrobe, and seek it out from eco-ethical brands that match your signature strengths.

12. Use your extra cash to donate to an eco fashion cause that you believe in; it will make you feel good.

13. Continue to do random acts of kindness for the environment, like cleaning up trash on the beach.

14. Address underlying needs about material possessions. What drives you to want what you want?

15. Be a leader among your friends. Play "What's on Your Back" and share all that you have learned in the ReFashion Workshop so that you can level up together.

Accountability

Reach out to your accountability partner and tell them about your experience with Sekhmet's Threads. Are you experiencing any factors that deter you from your goal of transformation? Have you overcome the need to tie knots and have ingrained new patterns? What is happening for you?

Journal

1. Reflect: What are your biggest struggles with committing to ReFashion? Post a message in the discussion group about what you are coming up against. How are you making ReFashioning your enemy? What bad habits are contributing to your unhealthy connection with fashion? What small steps can you take to start seeing ReFashioning as your ally?
2. Contemplate how you can naturally integrate "Making Fashion Your Ally" every day.
3. Meditate: In a quiet place where you won't be disturbed, sit with Sekhmet's Threads for ten minutes and contemplate the power of transformation. Let it sink into your hands as you hold the knots, and become one with your heart.

20

Veterinary

If fast fashion can be toxic to humans, you bet it is toxic for your pets and wild animals as well.

After learning that wildlife populations plummeted by 69% since 1970, I wanted to know if there is a connection between the fashion industry and the loss of wild animals. Sienna Martz at PETA had already taught me about the deforestation of the Amazon for cattle, aka, leather. But I wanted to know if domesticated animals could be harmed too.

So I went to the top animal toxicologist in the US to find out what is going on. Karyn Bischoff is head of the Toxicology Lab at Cornell University, and what she has to say informs us on a few scary and disturbing facts about animal toxicology, and it overlaps with how we care for our clothes.

I made a recording booth out of my bedroom closet at the beginning of COVID, and intended to make only audio recordings for my podcast. But it turns out people preferred to be face to face digitally. So I met with Professor Bischoff awkwardly surrounded by my wardrobe, which seemed appropriate somehow, and found her to be bubbly and bright with information on plastic.

"Well, I mean, I think everybody has seen the pictures of, you know, the albatrosses that are nesting on islands, feeding big chunks of plastic to their babies, because when they forage, they can't tell the difference between their normal prey and floating plastic. You've probably seen the pictures of the sea turtles that have choked on plastic bags. And you've heard all the stories about the whales that are beached and they're full of plastic. I think a few years ago, there was a really horrifying picture of a terrapin turtle that got stuck in a plastic soda ring, and it grew around the soda ring.

"So we know that plastic has caused some detrimental effects to wildlife. And we've known it for a really long time. I mean, we've known it since we were kids. Plastic really wasn't a big thing before the 1960s, so honestly, it's kind of crazy. Now when you think about it, you know, it was less than 100 years ago that people did not have plastic in their house.

"When I started studying plastic, one of the things that I found out, and I kind of, in the back of my mind knew this, because at the time, there was an Obama administration ruling that said, 'No microplastic beads in cosmetics.' Back then we had facial scrubs that had little bits of plastic that were a little bit abrasive and also the same with toothpaste that would help rub off the dead skin cells and tartar off your teeth. They were seeing these microbeads in water supplies. So that was really when people started wondering what happens to plastic after we use it. Besides just the big chunks of plastic strangling wildlife and things like that.

"What exactly is a microplastic? A microplastic is a piece of plastic that is less than half a centimeter in size. So 5 millimeters, what's that, probably about two-tenths of an inch or something like that, very, very small bit particles, but large enough that you can see them. But you know, anything about the size of a grain of rice or a lentil.

"Where does clothing come in? Well, if you look at the labels on your clothing, all the polyesters are made out of fossil materials.

"What are they doing to us? The general answer is, 'We don't know.' There are things that are used to make plastic more pliable, more sturdy, more this, more that. Those things might have effects on our bodies. They might be, for example, endocrine disruptors, they call them, which is when they affect the hormone system of your body via sexual hormones, or even normal hormones that you need, like insulin. We know that life comes in all different sizes, we have everything from tiny bacteria that you can see maybe with a very high-powered microscope. Then there's even things like mycoplasma that you need a super-high-powered microscope to see. And we know that there's small organisms like daphnia, the little water fleas, we all grew up looking at under the microscope. When you look in pond water and things like that, algae, little tiny single-celled organisms, small multicelled organisms, these creatures have to eat. They're finding that they can't really tell plastic from other food particles.

"I had a colleague here who studied fish, and she looked at a baby newborn fish, and their little intestines were full of plastic. So it causes them to not get enough nutrition; it can even cause impactions. It could basically block the system so they can't eat anymore. The other thing is these plastics are really... I'm trying to figure out how to explain the chemistry as easily as possible. But in chemistry, like attracts like; for example, oil and water; you mix oil and water or mix vinegar and water to make your salad dressing and it always separates because they are different chemically. The water and vinegar are different from the oils. Because plastics come from oil. Remember, it's a petrochemical. It attracts other things that are miscible. In oils, and a lot of the insecticides we use, and a lot of the chemical contaminants from back in the old days like

DDT, like PCBs, polychlorinated biphenyls — now we're talking about the perfluorooctanoic acid PFOAs, and other compounds like that, from, you know, Teflon products and things like that — those are fat soluble also. So are some heavy metals like mercury.

"So if they're fat soluble, they're plastic soluble. So if we're ingesting these things, is it possible that we're getting contaminated from them, we're getting small doses of contaminants when we eat them? I don't know; the other possibility, of course, is because the plastics do take up liquid-type substances, liquid-loving substances, maybe they're taking them out of our body; maybe they go through and they say, 'Oh, there's a PVC molecule, I'm gonna bind to that, and take them out.' We don't actually know; it could really go either way. Some other things that kind of follow: So we know that when big chunks of macroplastic break down to less than half a centimeter, less than 5 millimeters, then it's microplastic. Okay, what happens when the microplastics break down? Because they don't biodegrade either. It doesn't. They don't reach some size threshold, and then just kind of cease to exist. They just keep getting smaller, and smaller, and smaller, and smaller.

"Now they're talking about something called nanoplastic, and nanoplastic is much smaller than a human blood cell. I mean, it is not something you would see on a normal microscope. It's tiny. I mean, we're talking the size of a virus particle at this point — very, very small. How are they interacting with ourselves? I mean, they could definitely go back and forth through a cell membrane, because cell membranes are fat. As we know, plastic kind of likes to interact with that. So it's something, you know, that's something that's just coming into the scientific culture right now. But they're going to not know. But the other problem, of course, that we have is if you stop, and I try to avoid polyester, I don't use much rayon, but I try to avoid polyesters. And acrylics, even though I still have some clothes from the eighties that are polyester that are still in perfect condition, because polyester is forever." She paused to take a breath.

"That is terrifying to think about," I said. "Really, plastic is carrying toxins straight into our bodies, and the bodies of animals in the ecosystem. How can our relationship with our clothes affect our pets at home?"

"So yeah," she started again. "A lot of the products that we use, especially cleaning products, laundry detergents, even fabric softeners that people put around their house, you need to watch out for detergents with your pets.

"This actually ties in kind of nicely with the plastics because plastics are lipophilic. They like fat. And detergents are made to get rid of fat, right, you remember, 'Oh, which was the laundry detergent that's said to take grease stains out?' So basically, what these detergents do is they break down the fat by attacking it. These tend to be long molecules and one side is water soluble, and one side is fat soluble. So the fat-soluble part sticks to the dirt on the clothing. And the water-soluble part gets washed away in the water. So it basically takes that fat, that dirt, off your clothing and into the water. And that's how it works. And that's how the soap you use in your hands works.

"Intro to Cell Biology 101. The inside of a cell is water, and the surface of the cell is fat. So when your cells contact detergent, oh, it binds to the membrane on the surface of the cells which are made out of fat, just like it would bind to the dirt. I always had kind of a potty mouth. So, I did ingest a lot of soap as a child! My mother wasn't just like 'The bar of your soap in your mouth,' she was like 'Bite, bite into it, I want to see tooth marks when I pull it out of your mouth.' You know, I did it. So you know a small amount of soap ingestion probably isn't gonna hurt you. A lot of these detergents, they cause damage to your tissues, they cause these chemical burns by dissolving the cells, literally dissolving the surface of the cells.

"The thing about pets is they don't tend to wash their hands all the time. So if you get something on the outside of a cat or a dog on its paws, it's gonna end up inside that animal eventually, because they're going to groom it with their mouth. That's how they function. Especially cats. Cats are really fastidious about that. And the really important thing with cats and dogs is the way their toes are structured, they kind of are kept together. They don't spread out their fingers like we do, they have their toes kind of stuck together. So you have to make sure you get in between all of the toes really, really well with water. Because if you don't, then you will get burns in between where the toes contact each other because that's where the detergent will stay.

"I do diagnostics for poisoned animals. With the top ten cat poisons, laundry detergents are number three. And that makes sense, right? Because cats like knocking stuff over. It's what they do. And they like climbing counters, especially counters they know they're not supposed to be on. You know, when you tell the dog 'Don't do something' that dogs like, okay, don't do that. When you tell a cat not to do something the cat likes, she'll do it while you're not looking.

"The other aspect related to care of clothing that I want to bring up that has been a concern of many, many years is one of dry cleaning. Dry cleaning is done everywhere around the world. And by the way, my discussion is not just limited to the US; we're talking about the global impacts of this powerful industry worldwide. You will find that the dry cleaning industry uses a number of chemicals, and it has evolved. Just starting off we're using hydrocarbons, for example, to using carbon tetrachloride, which is very, very toxic. And those have been phased out. But you know, recently they're still using things like perchloroethylene, which is one of the most commonly used chemicals in dry cleaning. Some people call it tetrachloroethylene. So, these are volatile compounds. And they can affect the brain's central nervous system, because inhalation of the fumes kind of just mimics, you know, drinking a little too much alcohol. So depression, nervous system depression, ataxia could be some of the effects — all the way to its effects on the kidneys and liver. The liver is particularly susceptible because it tends to want to break down these compounds. And in the process, it could be affected, but because these compounds are volatile they also affect the respiratory system.

"These chemicals get into the air and the alleyways around the dry-cleaning building and into the waterways where it can harm undomesticated animals that drink city water and can cause harm for any animal that comes in contact with it.

"So in review, it's fat-soluble plastic that could be killing off wild animals on land and sea, it's messy toxic detergents poisoning your pets, and it's dry-cleaning compounds poisoning animals that roam in population centers. Make no mistake, we are harming animals with our apparel."

Professor Bischoff and I discussed so much more in that interview, and you can listen to it on my podcast *Environmental Style Now* for the full story. Our talk reminded me again of the planet being a person, Mother Earth, and how the explosion of chemicals we have created for synthetic apparel, flame retardants and softeners, and for cleaning our clothes is poisoning precious life. We are the cause of this suffering. So how do we get out of this cycle? With the fourth and final Noble Truth of ReFashion.

The Fourth Noble Truth of ReFashion

In review, the Four Noble Truths of ReFashion are a way for us to level up to heightened awareness of our interconnectedness, and our role as stewards of the planet. Each step is designed to awaken understanding of your past habits and ascribe new practices that you can use to find new levels of joy as you reshape your relationship with fashion.

- The First Noble Truth of ReFashion: Our planet is suffering.
- The Second Noble Truth of ReFashion: The cause of suffering is desire, greed, and the delusion of separation — our sense of not being enough.
- The Third Noble Truth of ReFashion is the end of suffering — waking up from the trance of separation, the small sense of self, the body of fear, and connecting to the global self.
- The Fourth Noble Truth of ReFashion is the oath to the end of suffering — the Threefold Path of Give/Take/Story.

The final Noble Truth is the prescription for the end of suffering for the planet. This is a set of principles that create the Threefold Path: Give/Take/Story.

I've introduced this to you before to prime you for taking it in as a way of living. If you really take it to heart, you will see what is outside yourself as a mirror of the inside of yourself. Your perception of the outside world is a reflection of your inner world. If you love and embrace yourself fully and are confident about your value, you will see love and perceive goodness in the world outside you. And it comes in three forms that are not to be taken in any order, but rather support and reinforce one another.

1. Give of yourself sustainably: All that comes from within that is extended without — an outward pouring of thoughts, objects, actions, ideas, and relationships. Giving sustainably can be sharing what you have learned from this book about eco-ethical fashion; it can be how you give your clothing back to the Earth from whence it came; it can be how you give your time. You are called to stay awake and be aware of what you give of yourself. Because what you give to the world will attract what you

receive from it. And when you awaken to your inherent and unconditional value, you will begin to attract exactly what you want. There is spiritual giving and physical giving. I challenge you to choose the highest vibration for both so that you may receive the highest value of both.

2. Take from the world sustainably: All that comes from without that is taken within — what you receive both spiritually and physically. It is an accumulation of materials, media, ideas, love, and whatever else comes from the outside that is taken in. Receiving sustainably in a spiritual way looks like using your inner wisdom and discretion to let only the highest vibrations of love into your life. Because you deserve it. Stop letting in people who drop their weight on you or give you anxiety. Start allowing yourself to receive the eternal love of the universe. It is vast. Taking sustainably in the physical world means buying for yourself materials that have been made with integrity and care for people and the planet. All that you choose to take from the world around you should be taken with love, discretion, and goodwill. So that when it reaches your heart, you can then solidify within yourself your story.

3. Incorporate sustainability into your story: All that self-talk that goes on in the back of your mind — this is where we form the stories about ourselves. It is where you claim ownership, and form your identity. The story you choose for yourself also has a vibration that affects the outer world. You can select your thoughts just the same way you select your clothes every day. Your story creates the framework for the reality that you are going to live. Making sustainability a part of your identity means you claim it for yourself, and you act in alignment with your beliefs. This part is key in your role as a steward of

the planet. By living in line with your beliefs, you show others what it can be like. You become an example. And the story you tell to others becomes the real you. Think wisely. See high vibrations. And when you have done the work to solidify a story that manifests giving of your highest self spiritually and physically, you will then receive or take the highest forms spiritually and physically. All three parts of the Threefold Path begin interacting in unison.

The Three Stages are totally intertwined, and together they are the path towards the end of suffering for the planet as far as humans can contribute. The more you place love in the cycle of the Threefold Path, the more abundant your state of mind becomes, because you are feeding into a cycle that sustains itself. In your inner world, the love you give will come back to you, and then you will tell yourself the story that you are loved, and then it goes from you again. A trinity feeding itself continuously.

Here is how it could sound out loud: "From myself I give my sense of peace, and from others I accept their sense of peace, and so I confirm within myself, I am at peace."

On a physical level it could go like this: I tell a friend about how I learned that fashion is the second most polluting industry in the world, and I give her information. She then decides the next time she shops that she will not buy that polyester dress after all. Now her story and your stories become tied to sustainability, and it encourages you the next time you have the impulse to buy something fast.

In my life, I have chosen to practice all three stages with the creation of my company Holding Court. It is a way for me to give you all of this transformative information so that you can ReFashion to the next level, and to take an income for my work in creating an eco-ethical apparel line. My story is my own, but

I also create fictional stories that weave sustainability into every plotline. These are my most abundant commitments.

I would like for you to create your own commitments to end the suffering of the planet and evolve the way you interact with people and the environment. By naming thoughts and actions that you can achieve in all three stages, and putting them into practice with the help of reflection, contemplation, and meditation, you will finally achieve total ReFashioning. You will have reconditioned your body, mind, and soul to become a steward of this precious planet.

Give

In your journal, write down five ways in which you can give of yourself in a more sustainable way in regard to your fashion habits. Be creative. Maybe you can give advice on where to shop from eco-ethical brands; maybe you can give a friend something from your "Trade" pile from your closet purge.

When you write your actions down, state your name first:

I, _____, am going to give sustainably by _____.

If you wish to, expand this even more. Make a commitment to give more lovingly of your attention to your friends and family. Or to give more compassionately to your own health. Imagine a positive leap in the way you give, and write it down and commit to it.

Take

Now think of five creative ways you can consume more sustainably. This can be choosing to purchase from a brand that has a zero waste policy, or to watch more documentaries about eco living instead of binge-watching your normal programming.

I, _____, am going to take sustainably by _____.

A step further, imagine how you can take more sustainably in your entire lifestyle. What can you eat that will leave less of an impact? How can you be more receptive to your friends and family? You can make a positive leap in the way you take in every form possible. Let the imagination go wild, and write down a few ideas you have. Commit to them.

Story

Your new identity as a steward and protector of the planet. This one takes a little time, but be honest with yourself. Write down a few sentences that sum up who you want to be, now that you know how damaging fashion is to people and the planet. What does it mean to you to be a steward? Try to keep it as short and sweet as possible. For example:

> I, _____, am a steward and protector of the planet because I am aware of my role in the give/take of the universe, and aim to channel only what is positive and sustainable.

Over time, this little sentence will become a part of your personal story, and it will reinforce your actions as you become more mindful of how you give and how you take. With all three in play, it will be easier for you to walk in alignment with your highest integrity. Imagine a time in the future when the Threefold Path is so integrated, you don't have to think about it anymore. You simply will become a steward and protector of the planet and its people because it feels good; it feels right.

Write your Story Statement on a sticky note, or on a piece of paper where you can see it daily as you get ready in the morning. This positive affirmation is a little reminder of all the work you have done to get here, and will help you walk your new truth every day.

Accountability

What you just did above is a beautiful thing. Words are powerful, especially when you write them down. But ReFashioning your very identity will not be an overnight thing. You will make mistakes; you will fight tightly ingrained habits that convince you to fill your emptiness with a quick click on Shein. It isn't about perfection. Love is greater than the pressure to be perfect. Love is acceptance. It is kindness. It is freedom, and it is beauty. Love is forgiveness as well. Forgive yourself for not giving of yourself sustainably, for not receiving or taking sustainably, and for harmful stories you have told yourself. You have everything you need inside when you pause and let go of the need to be perfect.

Take it one step further and share your [Threefold Path] with the community forum in the online class. Words are powerful. Your unique outlook on stewardship may inspire others to deepen their truth and may enlighten you to other ways you can Give, Take, and Tell Your Story sustainably.

While you're at it, take a moment and thank someone for their contribution. Call it an action of gratitude.

Journal

1. Reflect: The Threefold Path works together in unison like a triangle always running into itself at each corner. How do your new commitments run into each other to fulfill the Fourth Noble Truth of ReFashion — the end of the suffering of the planet?
2. Contemplate the power of your new identity. Let it rest deep within a corner of your heart that no one can touch. This is yours.
3. Meditate: For ten minutes in a quiet place where no one will bother you, sit with your legs crossed and your eyes closed. Your breath will calm you as you follow it in and

out, allowing it to empty your mind and focus on clarity of mind. Take your Story Statement with you, and repeat it to yourself, relaxing into the message until it feels like it is part of the background.

21

Washing

There are 8 billion of us. If we each do one little thing, it makes a huge impact.
— Ian Somerhalder, actor and United Nations Ambassador on *E.S.Now* podcast

Of all the modern luxuries that harm the environment, we almost never hear about washing machines. And frankly, I understand why. Owning a washing machine in many places in the world is a mark of making it; it is a privilege to be able to forgo the hours it takes to handwash clothing. When I lived in a bungalow in LA without a washer or dryer on the property, I often set aside a full afternoon to handwash all of my laundry in the bathtub, hanging it to dry on the fire escape — all of the time desperately wishing I could just throw it into a machine and be done with it. Most people in the developed world operate their households with these little helpers, and they are blissfully ignorant of the horrendous impact washing machines have on our oceans.

I give it back to Karyn Bischoff, department head of toxicology, to explain why.

"With every wash, hundreds of thousands of microfibers are released into the environment — a 6 kg wash could produce up to 700,000 fibers. I mean, we're talking 100 million fibers in a week's load of laundry or something crazy like that. I mean, just high, high numbers of little bits of fiber are going out into the environment.

"And then to make matters worse, you take your clothes out of the washing machine, and what do you do? You put them in the dryer, and you maybe put in a dryer sheet which is made out of wet plastic, in with your clothes to tumble. You've seen the lint trap in your dryer that's got all these little particles. So that gives you some idea of how much of these fibers there are, and actually that's only a portion of it. But some of this stuff makes it through your filter, the very tiny particles, and they go out into the air.

"So now you're breathing them too. So now it's in your food, it's in your water. They've actually discovered that in cities in metropolitan areas, there's a lot of plastic pollution in the air, and it's between fibers from clothing, bits of tires. When there's a high-traffic area the tires do wear down, and little bits of the tire can become aerosolized and kind of suspended as dust particles in the air. They blend in with the clothing fibers and stick to surfaces. So that's another major source in some of these cities. So these things are everywhere."

I can attest to the black grime that builds up on surfaces in Los Angeles when I leave my windows open. Imagining that in my lungs... I mean, clothing fibers and aerosolized tires? The thought of it is incredibly disturbing. How can that not cause harm?

So what can we do to cut back on creating harmful microplastic and using chemical detergents?

"First of all, you likely don't need to wash your clothes as often as you are. Sure, certain articles of clothing need to be as fresh as possible for sanitary reasons, but jeans, T-shirts, jackets, sweaters... Most other clothes can be worn at least three times before you need to wash them. And when you go to wash them, you can help prevent 85% of fiber shedding by washing it all in a Guppyfriend bag. It's a zippered mesh bag that keeps your clothes pressed together while they wash. Machine washing easily distresses the weave of the fibers in your clothes, so if you machine wash, use a Guppyfriend or an off-brand to prevent shedding, and wash it on the delicate cycle, always."

In episode 24 of my podcast *E.S.Now*, Ian Somerhalder adds, "What would really help with reducing energy consumption is to wash clothes with cold water, and to do it before peak hours. Before 9 a.m. Between noon and 2 p.m. is good."

Here are some simple solutions you can start doing for stain removal and a recipe for natural nontoxic laundry detergent.

Stain Removal 101

When a stain happens, immediately soak it in cold water so it doesn't set, then treat is as recommended below:

- Red wine: Soak red wine stains in white wine, then cover with baking soda, let sit, and rinse.
- Foundation: Grab some shaving cream and gently work it into the stain with a washcloth.
- Chocolate: Flush the back of the stain with cold water, dab with liquid dishwashing detergent, and let soak.
- Lipstick: Scrape off any excess lipstick and saturate the stain with non-aerosol hairspray, then dab carefully to remove.
- Grass: Soak in white vinegar, then scrub gently with a toothbrush and liquid dishwashing detergent.
- Deodorant: Gently blot it away with a damp paper towel.

DIY Nontoxic Detergent Recipe

Ingredients:

- 1 cup of baking soda
- ⅓ cup of sea salt
- 2½ cups of warm water
- 1 cup of liquid castile soap
- Water as needed to fill a gallon jug
- Essential oil of choice (lavender is lovely, and safe for pets; do your research)

Instructions:

- Add the baking soda, sea salt, and the warm water to the gallon jug.
- Shake the jug until the salt and baking soda dissolve.
- Add the castile soap and fill the gallon jug with water.
- Move the jug gently to mix.

How to use:

- If you have a traditional washing machine, use half a cup or a full cup of laundry detergent, depending on the size of the load.
- For high-efficiency washing machines, we recommend using only a quarter of a cup per regular load, and half a cup if you want to wash more clothes in one load.

Pro tip:

- A natural fabric softener that you already have lying around the house is apple cider vinegar.
- Add half a cup before the last rinse cycle while washing.

Putting It All into Action

After weeks of activities, practicing reflection, contemplation, and meditation, you have a full picture of the complete life of your garments — where on Earth the raw materials came from, where it was made, how it can be cared for, and how it can go back to the Earth. The Fourth Noble Truth presented you with the way to end the suffering of the planet and its people using the Threefold Path – Give/Take/Story. You have made it your goal to live in awareness as you give, take, and tell your personal story from now on.

To make the probability of your follow-through even stronger, we are going to hack your goals and make them achievable in the most scientific way possible.

Goal Setting

Gabriele Oettingen, an academic, psychologist, and professor of psychology at New York University and the University of Hamburg, has coined a method that will help you better achieve your goals called "WOOP."

That is:

- W — Wishing: visualization
- O — Outcome: what is the best outcome?
- O — Obstacles that may arise
- P — Plan: your if-then plan

"WOOP is a science-based mental strategy that people can use to find and fulfill their wishes, set preferences, and change their habits," says the Woop Your Life website. "WOOP is based on twenty years of scientific research. The method has been shown to be effective in numerous studies with people of all ages and in many areas of life."

Using this strategy, you can achieve goals both short term and long term. And you can use it for any part of your life:

interpersonal relationships, business, health, spirituality... you name it. Let's walk through each step of WOOP to see what it offers.

WOOP

Set ten minutes aside for this practice.

- What is your wish? Write down what your wish is, and how long you think it will take to achieve it. This should be something challenging that you can realistically fulfill.
- What is the best outcome to fulfilling your wish? How would fulfilling your wish make you feel? Take a moment and fully imagine that outcome.
- Identify your obstacles. What is it within you that holds you back from fulfilling your wish? What is it in you that stands in the way of your wish? What is your main inner obstacle? Take a moment and imagine your obstacles. Imagine them fully.
- Make an if-then plan. What can you do to overcome your obstacles? Name one action you can take or one thought you can make to overcome an obstacle. "If _____, then I will _____." Slowly repeat it to yourself.

This is a wildly successful tool if you commit to using it every morning for the duration of the time you believe it will take to fulfill your goal. Determining obstacles and planning your way out sets you up for a path forward. And the results are real.

Thirty-Day WOOP Challenge and Fashion Fast

This is aimed to set you up for success as you move on from ReFashioning. Your goal might be to live out the Threefold Path – Give/Take/Story – but things will, as always, get in your way. And you need a plan set in place for when you lose focus.

Go ahead and get out your journal. Open to a fresh page and prepare to WOOP your ReFashion commitment to success.

1. W: Wishing, visualization. What wishes do you have for your lifestyle following the end of this workbook? Consider your ReFashion commitment from the last chapter.
2. O: Outcome. What is the best outcome you can achieve for your wish?
3. O: Obstacles may arise. What are they?
4. P: Plan your if-then statement. "If my obstacle _____ arises, then I will _____."

On a sticky note, write "WOOP" wherever you do your meditations. This will help you remember this action first thing in the morning before you start your day.

If you are interested in testing the theory beyond ReFashion, by all means download a [WOOP] Kit from the creators by following the link in the ReFashion Online Workshop.

And finally, now that you have narrowed down your personal style and have ideas for what brands you might want to invest with in the future, take a pause. There is no rush to buy anything that you don't need. Instead of filling in that space immediately, sit with the space for a 30-day fashion fast. This will give you enough time to know what you really need next before you accidentally indulge in compulsive buying of eco-ethical clothes. We want you to have all the faculties of your awareness ready, and a 30-day fashion fast is a healthy reset.

So go and mark your calendar! You have a month to chill out.

Journal

1. Reflect: Have you ever done a 30-day fashion fast? How do past impulse buys inform you on what you can

expect of your self-control? Do you need to ask your accountability partner to keep you in check?

2. Contemplate how it feels when obstacles no longer have their power. When things that seem hard simply morph into practice.

3. Meditate: In a quiet place where no one will bother you, sit for ten minutes with your eyes closed in a cross-legged position. Breathe in deeply, and slowly, letting it become regular. Focus your thought on the breath as it moves in and out, and feel through your body with your breath, starting at the base of your spine. Find where there are points of tension, places where energy is blocked, and breathe love and light into it, moving into your lower abdomen, up into the belly, and move it into your heart. Wherever there is a blockage, breathe in more love and light; imagine all of the movement is pure. Move it up into your throat, and then behind your eyes. Take your time to breathe into your crown, allowing it to pour out of your head and surround you in light. The light moves below and comes up again through the base of the spine as a torus — an uninterrupted movement with no beginning and no end.

22

Unsustainable

In order for us to change we need to change the roots, the system itself.

— Adrian Grenier, actor and activist

My phone rang for the fourth time that day. I saw the name on my screen and placed my thumb to answer the red dot even though every part of me wanted to throw my device against the wall. My investor was calling, and that meant for the next hour and a half I was obligated to say, "Yeah, sure," and, "Umm... I don't think that's accurate, but okay," until eventually saying, "That's a great idea, let's give it a try" while trying to ensure the business was still moving ahead.

With this investor, I had already become accustomed to giving him five to six hours of my time daily, acquiescing to things that I didn't agree with; ideas so bizarre that I couldn't help but laugh half the time (like have MMA champion Holly Holm pair up with Blue Man Group, paint her blue, and then somehow make it about eco fashion; or make the new Victoria's Secret Runway spinoff about saving the ocean by centering it on fish-themed fashion), but I felt obligated to follow every dead end. I bent my morals. I bent my comfort zone. I had a friendship poisoned, and a romantic partner driven away. And the very last straw was what could be described as a #metoo moment involving a minor. Needless to say, my first foray into owning a sustainable fashion company was not sustainable.

It can happen to the best of us, and that is just microeconomics. Let's talk about macroeconomics. What have we learned so far about the fashion industry?

- The majority of fabric we use is created from a toxic nonrenewable resource: fossil fuels.
- We have learned that one in six people on the planet work in the fashion industry, many without receiving a living wage.
- 80% of those workers are women.
- The fashion industry is responsible for 10% of carbon emissions, and that is on the rise.
- The fashion industry contributes 20% of all water pollution.
- Toxic chemicals from clothing seep into your body.
- 85% of our clothes end up in the landfill.

I also failed to mention that at the moment, we simply aren't making enough renewable fabrics to clothe the 8 billion people on the planet. Clean artisan fabrics like the Ahimsa silk we talked about with Carroll Dunham or the hemp we went over with Courtney Moran are either not scalable, or they are decades away from being the norm because of bureaucratic red tape.

All of these factors combined paint a grim picture of a truly unsustainable industry. It simply cannot keep going the way that it is. It is a humanitarian and environmental disaster.

So what can we implement right now that could create critical change in the entire lifespan of the fashion industry? The buzzword is "circular fashion."

Circular fashion gets its roots from the novel concept of a circular economy. The idea is that anything that we manufacture or create can then be recycled instead of thrown away. Everything becomes a renewable resource.

Key points according to circular fashion:

- Use fewer materials when producing individual items for increased recyclability.
- Work to remove nonrecyclable and polluting materials from the supply chain.
- Recapture everything, from garment offcuts to packaging for reuse.
- Ensure use and reuse for as long as possible, including collection schemes and bringing the recycled materials back to a "good as new" state.
- Return any unavoidable waste to nature safely.

In my own life, I have considered how to get rid of old clothes that are rags and tags. I have thought about how I could use an old linen skirt in my planter bed to hold down seeds. But the more I think about it, it would be much more impactful to use that same fabric and put it back into the system to create a brand-new skirt instead of growing a new plant. Circular fashion has a unique edge because you're simply using materials that already exist. The carbon footprint is substantially less.

To make circular fashion possible, you would need to design fabrics with recyclability in mind from conception. Consider what happens when you take a sweater that has wool, polyester, and rayon in it, in different percentages. To recycle something like that... we just don't have the technology. But if we designed for recyclability, then we would invent compatible fabrics, and it would come with a label that would help consumers know where to deposit it at the end of its life.

There is technology that already exists with a company called Circular Fashion, and they have designed a simple system where the designer buys a recycled fabric from their website, it comes with a QR code that tells the consumer where and how to drop it off when they want to discard it, and it's able to be sorted into the proper recycling process once it is received at a recycling station.

They are just one company, but this is something that we could do on a global scale, starting tomorrow if we wanted to. Because it doesn't require 100,000 hectares of land, alien technology, or redesigning the wheel. A circular fashion economy is the closest thing we have to a sustainable fashion economy.

Imagine it as infinite energy. Our current way of discarding fabrics at the end of their life sends them to a place where they melt and blend and compress with all of the other junk we throw away — sofas, roof tiles, oat milk containers — it's all getting smashed together and buried under dirt. Have you ever been to a landfill? Landfills are troublesome places that are practically going to be no-man's land for the rest of our time on this planet simply because of how toxic that soup is.

Using circular fashion, all of the energy, the photosynthesis of the plant cells, goes on to become something new again and again until it simply disintegrates. Ideally we are choosing only plant fibers here, but for now it would be a good use of fantastic plastic polyester if we could use it till we phase it out. Infinite, sustainable energy... this is a reality we could start living tomorrow.

Given there aren't that many stations for recycling clothing set up right now, what do you do with your clothes when you are done with them? After all this time, we are finally going to open up your closet and make room for the new.

Closet Purge

One of the fastest ways to change your life is to open up space. To create space for the new, you have to shed some of the old.

Shedding styles that no longer serve you will get you closer to the new style that wants to break through. Your eco style.

1. Before you determine what is serving you, it's best to organize. Designate four areas for the clothes you are discarding: Fix, Donate, Trade, Sell. Having designated areas will make the process happen more quickly, and keep you sane while you go through years of the old you.

2. Go through one section of your wardrobe at a time. Be ruthless; less is more. You will be surprised at how little of your closet you actually wear. Determine if it is out of date for you, too worn, too similar to something else, never worn, or something you can never bring yourself to wear. Focus on what brings you joy and what meets your needs regarding life's complexities. Narrow it down to what is in the best shape and what feels like the style you are heading toward.

3. If you find items you love but don't quite fit you right, or it has something damaged that can be repaired, toss it in the "Fix" pile. You may be able to have it tailored or repaired.

4. For items you don't want that are a little worn, or even things that nobody can wear, add it to the "Donate" pile. The great thing about donating to Goodwill, Salvation Army, and similar nonprofits — aside from a tax break — is that they have built-in systems for textile items that cannot be resold. They will sort through what is salvageable, and donate what would have ended up in a landfill to companies that shred the fabric into emergency blankets, car insulation, and more. Never throw your clothes in the garbage.

5. "Trade" will be fun. For things that you don't imagine you will wear, but kind of want to see again, trade them with your friends. You get to give them something of you,

and in return you get something new to you that was precious to them. Pretty good!

6. The "Sell" pile is great because it has the potential to earn you something back for your investment. You can list your items on a number of online stores like Etsy, Poshmark, Craigslist even, and if you want to move your closet fast you can send an entire bag, postage covered, to thredUP where they will sell it for you and give you a portion of the profit. Up to you! Or you can always go the old-fashioned way and have a yard sale.

7. As you put items back, organize them in a way that satisfies you. Maybe it's by color, or season, or it could be by designer. Make it so that your mind is at ease whenever you open a drawer or peek into a closet. Take a moment and savor the room for change that you just created.

To make things a little easier ahead of time, prepare for the purge by creating an account with thredUP via this link on the ReFashion Workshop online page: [Closet Purge]. They will send you a prepaid postage garment bag for all the items you can resell. If you enter this code when you sign up, you will get 30% off at Holding Court for later use.

Accountability

Go ahead and reach out to your accountability partner and tell them what you accomplished today. What did you get rid of that was difficult to let go of? What did you keep that still brings you joy? How does it feel to have space?

Journal

1. Reflect on the styles you kept. Do they suit your signature strengths? How does it feel to be lighter?

2. Contemplate the success of preparing your home for your transformation. Pat yourself on the back for fulfilling this necessary step in walking the walk of planetary stewardship.

3. Meditate: In a quiet place where no one will distract you, cross your legs and close your eyes for ten minutes. Follow your breath into your chest, and breathe space into it. Continue to breathe, feeling how much room there is inside amid all the psychic energy you store. Let yourself settle into that space, breathing more deeply. Sit in this space for as long as you can, letting it open more and more with each breath, leaving you open and free.

23

Generations X, Y, and Z

If you have gotten all the way here, to the end, and you still haven't been able to pin down your buying habits with honesty — sometimes the truth eludes us — there are people on the case tracking each of these super-consuming generations, and this can help guide us out.

According to *The True Cost*, the world now consumes about 80 billion new pieces of clothing every year. This is 400% more than the amount we consumed just two decades ago. As new clothing comes into our lives, we also discard it at a shocking pace. The average American now generates 82 pounds of textile waste each year. That adds up to more than 11 million tons of textile waste from the US alone. Historically, clothing has been something we have held on to for a long time, but with cheap clothing now abundantly available we are beginning to see the things we wear as disposable.

Generations X, Y, and Z are the biggest consumers to date. And to shed a little light on each generation, head of marketing and market research Kasi Martin of Fairtrade USA has broken down each generation's contribution and how they can do better now.

"Gen X is sort of a forgotten generation," she says, "but the trends I see with them is that they are very sophisticated and educated. Thirty-five percent of Gen X-ers hold degrees, as compared to Millennials, or Gen Y at 17%. They are very loyal so they tend to still shop at department stores. And they are loyal to heritage brands like Nike or Gap.

"Members of Generation X face the biggest challenge of breaking rank and finding new brands and new ways to shop. For Gen X, I recommend finding your local brick-and-mortar mom-and-pop eco-store in town and becoming a loyal patron. You will get that same feeling you are used to, going to the department store, only it will be better for the planet.

"My generation, Generation Y, is still coming off of fast fashion," Martin says. "Now that we have more information, Millennials really care. And we have more spending power so we can make change. We are the nostalgic vintage buyers. Millennials are the buyers of independent brands and tend to lean into an experience and authenticity rather than just a mannequin in a shop window. But they also want value. Millennials are the biggest spenders of all thus far.

"Millennials have an interesting place in the market. Having grown up just at the beginning of the digital age, we were mall rats and were eager subscribers to LiveJournal and Myspace when they launched. The internet was basically modeled for this generation, but they enjoy seeing and finding culture as well. Just take your search a little further, don't wait for it to come to you. Take that need for experience and make this journey of ReFashioning your new discovery mission.

"Gen Z," says Martin, "they are the social buyers. They are all on social media and are all about showing you their life. They love tons of color and are incredibly, incredibly savvy. I think they are going to outsmart all of the Millennials.

"What we need to remember about Gen Z is that they are the most photographed generation of all time. We need to be cognizant of it because it can really influence their buying habits. They are going to always want new outfits for pictures. They won't want to be seen in the same thing for their pictures. So they feel a lot of pressure to buy new clothes to set themselves out from the crowd because social media is so saturated for them. That's why you are seeing a proliferation of intense color and overstyling.

"That's the Gen Z-ers, whereas Millennials started the craze of brandless and no tags, no labels. So it's very different.

"So if we compare Gen Z-ers with the rise of sustainable fashion, it's going to be a really interesting mashup with shopping. There will be a lot more rentals, a lot of resale — it's already happening. They can create a new look, but it may be something used or borrowed. Style goes round in circles (even if the industry is not yet circular) and the nineties is cool again, so who needs to buy new? Be disruptive. Your voice is a powerful tool. Together we can demand change, clean up the mess. Say, 'Slow down, we have enough.'"

The Afterglow

As we reach the end of this book, you have hopefully gained significant insight into yourself and the world at large. You have listened to what the experts have to say, and have taken accountability for your participation in the lifespan of your garments. Through self-discovery and commitments, you have made incredible progress regarding your personal integrity in relation to the planet. And the planet thanks you.

As you move forward from here, take with you those little tips on enhancing your happiness through savoring, gratitude, and spending your money on experiences and things that align with your commitments as a steward of the planet.

And now that you have taken the time to recondition your brain through weeks of reflection, contemplation, and meditation, take with you your Story Statement and your WOOP plan to pull off the Threefold Path — Give/Take/Story. Leave your sticky notes in plain sight until you no longer need them. It could be six weeks, it could be six months. Let it sink into all aspects of your life and see how giving love in one area brightens up another.

You have learned that you don't need to sacrifice style for convenience. You are now aware. Buying cheap synthetic clothes made without consideration for the preservation of humanity would be a reflection of your disregard for people and the planet. You are more respectful than that. You live in a higher vibration.

Social Connection

I'll leave you with one last tip for your own happiness and well-being that can be a tool for your new identity as a steward of the planet. Add "eco fashion activist" to your "Give" stage in the Threefold Path, and connect with more people.

Research shows that when we create close ties with people, we are less vulnerable, and we are more likely to survive a near-fatal illness and less likely to fall prey to stressful events.

We tend to shy away from new encounters because we think maybe we don't have anything valuable to say, or we might annoy the person next to us. Not so! People who are engaged with by well-meaning strangers report more happiness after the encounter as well. Simply by being with other people, we boost our happiness.

Shared experiences take the cake. You are way more likely to find joy sharing your new love for eco-ethical fashion by connecting with other people who do too. If you decide to make eco fashion a conversation starter, you will suddenly find yourself happier for the fact that you are in a social connection with someone, and because you have valuable information to share that impacts the lives of everyone on the planet. It's another win-win for eco fashion!

Try it out and see how it feels. Talk to a stranger about the book you read, or about your recent closet purge. See if they are receptive; see if your integrity shines through.

Take it a step further and find other ways to get involved. There are activist groups, designers, and research studies who are begging for help on this cause. With so much room for innovation, we could really use another awakened mind to take action.

PERMA, Round 2

You have changed quite a bit about your life since you first took the PERMA Profiler. You have practiced reflection, contemplation, and meditation regularly. You have created your personal statement for the Threefold Path – Give/Take/Story — and are using WOOP to achieve your goals. And your closet has a whole lot of room for an eco-ethical future!

Let's see how much your well-being has changed since you began to ReFashion your life. In the online ReFashion Workshop, click the [Happiness Survey] and take the PERMA Profiler one more time.

Accountability

- In the ReFashion Workshop, report your final PERMA score in comparison to your first test at [PERMA vs. PERMA].
- Follow up with a [Commentary] on what you thought about the ReFashion Workbook. I'd love to hear about your experience now that you have completed it.
- Tell your accountability partner about the change in your PERMA results. Consider what changed and tell them what you think affected your test this time.

Journal

What is your new score on the PERMA test?

a. Positive emotions =
b. Engagement =

c. Relationships =

d. Meaning =

e. Accomplishment =

f. Health =

g. Negative emotions =

h. Loneliness =

i. Overall well-being =

1. Reflect on your experience of the ReFashion Workshop. What was the most effective practice for you to help you change your habits? What was the most challenging? What do you know now that you didn't before? How do you plan to share it?

2. Contemplate your new connection with the universe as a steward and protector of the planet and its people. Feel the potential in this identity, and what it means for your relationships with people.

3. The final meditation will be one of expansion. In a quiet place where you won't be interrupted, sit for ten minutes with your legs crossed and eyes closed. Breathe in deeply and let the breath inform your focus; follow it into your body wherever it needs to go. Just focus on the breath if thoughts arise. As you feel more free and open in your body, let the breath become a ball of light in your chest. Small at first, let it grow as you inhale, your body contracting on the exhale. It grows past the cavity of your chest, until it surrounds your entire body in a warm, gentle light. Breathe in again and let it fill the whole room with the love in your heart. As you breathe out, the light covers your entire house, and then your neighborhood, and then it covers your city in your love and connection. Breathe even deeper and it covers your country with your awareness and energy. One big breath, and you have enveloped the world in your presence of

light, love, and kindness. Stay for as long as you can hold it. And as you release, say "Thank you" for the mysterious gift of life and the role you get to play in it.

More Ways to Educate Yourself

Watch
- *Anthropocene* — www.anthropocenethemovie.com
- *Before the Flood* — Leonardo DiCaprio's documentary about the impact of climate change
- *China Blue* — a Teddybear Films documentary about two denim-factory workers in China
- *Cowspiracy* — a documentary about livestock farming and its enormous impact on the environment
- *I Am* — a documentary exploring what is wrong with the world and how can we make it better
- *Minimalism* — a documentary about how good it is to live with less
- *The True Cost* — Andrew Morgan's documentary on the garment industry's impact on people and the environment
- Volta — an online platform of inspiring videos on lifestyle, sustainability, and technology

Read
- *An Astronaut's Guide to Life on Earth* by Chris Hadfield
- *Sapiens: A Brief History of Humankind* by Yuval Noah Harari
- WWF. 2018. *Living Planet Report — 2018: Aiming Higher* by M. Grooten and R. E. A. Almond

.org
- Buycott — an app that scans barcodes for information about products
- Extinction Rebellion — an organization that uses civil disobedience to raise awareness about climate change

- Greenpeace: Detox Catwalk — an international organization that puts pressure on governments and corporations to protect the environment

Sell Your Clothes

- Buffalo Exchange — a brick-and-mortar chain that buys and sells in-season secondhand clothes
- Crossroads — a brick-and-mortar chain that buys and sells in-season secondhand clothes
- Designer-Vintage — buy and sell authentic designer apparel online
- Poshmark — the eBay of secondhand. Bid on designer clothes and sell your own at a price you determine.
- thredUP — the largest online consignment and thrift store. Sign up and they will send you a bag to fill with your unwanted but wearable clothes. Go shopping on store credit.

References

Chapter 1

Definition of Anthropocene
https://www.smithsonianmag.com/science-nature/what-is-the-anthropocene-and-are-we-in-it-164801414/

World Wide Fund for Nature, *Living Planet Report 2022*
https://livingplanet.panda.org/en-US/

Chapter 2

United Nations Zero Waste #ActNow
https://www.un.org/sustainabledevelopment/blog/2019/08/actnow-for-zero-waste-fashion/

Chapter 3

The Three Pillars of Sustainability
https://circularecology.com/sustainability-and-sustainable-development.html

The United Nations Sustainable Development Agenda
https://www.un.org/sustainabledevelopment/development-agenda/

Chapter 4

Greenpeace Detox Catwalk
https://wayback.archive-it.org/9650/20200401155311/http://p3-raw.greenpeace.org/international/en/campaigns/detox/fashion/detox-catwalk/

Chapter 5

Our World in Data
https://ourworldindata.org/emissions-by-sector

Chapter 7
Higg Materials Sustainability Index
https://howtohigg.org/higg-msi/

Chapter 8
Greenwash
https://greenwash.com/

Chapter 10
The How of Happiness
https://thehowofhappiness.com/

Chapter 11
Fashion Revolution Blue Jeans
https://www.fashionrevolution.org/about/transparency/

Chapter 12
UNICEF
https://labs.theguardian.com/unicef-child-labour/

Chapter 13
Fair Wear Foundation
https://www.fairwear.org/

"What's on Your Back" Map
https://www.minimumwage.com
https://www.tradeeconomics.com
https://globallivingwage.org/resource-library/

Chapter 14
Extinction Rebellion
https://rebellion.global/

Chapter 15

Lonely Whale
www.lonelywhale.org

Chapter 16

Red Carpet Green Dress
https://www.rcgdglobal.com/

Chapter 17

Waste
https://www.fashionrevolution.org/a-trail-of-plastic-waste-left-in-the-wake-of-uncontrolled-growth/

Chapter 18

Fast Fashion's Plastic Problem
https://www.thersa.org/reports/fast-fashions-plastic-problem

Made-By Environmental Benchmark for Fibers
https://www.researchgate.net/figure/The-MADE-BY-environmental-benchmark-fiber-classification-chart-Source-Common-objective_fig5_335139274

Chapter 22

Circular Fashion
https://circular.fashion/en/

Chapter 23

The *True Cost* Movie
https://truecostmovie.com/learn-more/environmental-impact/

About the Author

Courtney Barriger is a multifaceted artist, sustainability advocate, and award-winning creative. After experiencing the fast-fashion industry as an international model, she realized the need for a better way to make beautiful clothes and self-care goods that respect people and the planet. For over a decade, she has been working in sustainability as a lecturer, artist, fashion designer, and writer. Her work has a mystical edge that pushes the boundaries between nature, beauty, and responsibility, provoking conversation about the sociopolitical state of the planet.

Growing up on the beaches in Florida, Barriger has a rich connection with the natural world, which she draws inspiration from in her art. In 2018, she launched Holding Court, her eco-ethical brand that is dedicated to sustainability in fashion and consistently provokes conversation through art, film, and writing. Her zest for life and inherent curiosity have instilled in her a lust for wanting more and leaving no stone unturned.

When not on set or wordsmithing, she can be found traveling the world with nothing but a suitcase, or conspiring a new creative project. Barriger's passion for sustainability and art has made her a leading voice in the movement, and her work continues to inspire others to make a positive impact on the environment.

www.courtneybarriger.com

CHANGEMAKERS
BOOKS

Transform your life, transform our world. Changemakers
Books publishes books for people who seek to become
positive, powerful agents of change. These books inform,
inspire, and provide practical wisdom and skills to empower
us to write the next chapter of humanity's future.

www.changemakers-books.com